Magic Numbers for Consumer Marketing

Key Measures to Evaluate Marketing Success

Magic Numbers for Consumer Marketing

KEY MEASURES TO EVALUATE MARKETING SUCCESS

John Davis

John Wiley & Sons (Asia) Pte Ltd

3 1257 01571 6938

This publication is designed to provide accurate and authoritative information in regard to the subject matter covered. It is sold with the understanding that the publisher is not engaged in rendering professional services. If professional advice or other expert assistance is required, the services of a competent professional person should be sought.

Other Wiley Editorial Offices

John Wiley & Sons, 111 River Street, Hoboken, NJ 07030, USA
John Wiley & Sons, The Atrium Southern Gate, Chichester P019 8SQ, England
John Wiley & Sons (Canada) Ltd, 22 Worcester Road, Rexdale, Ontario M9W 1L1, Canada
John Wiley & Sons Australia Ltd, 33 Park Road (PO Box 1226), Milton, Queensland 4064, Australia
Wiley-VCH, Pappelallee 3, 69469 Weinheim, Germany

Library of Congress Cataloging-in-Publication Data

ISBN-13 978-0-470-82162-6
ISBN-10 0-470-82162-0

Typeset in 12/14 points, Times Roman by C&M Digitals (P) Ltd.
Printed in Singapore by Saik Wah Press Ltd
10 9 8 7 6 5 4 3 2

Contents

Introduction

As a career marketer, I have often wanted a shorthand guide to key marketing performance measures. Why? Several reasons: to improve planning sessions with my marketing teams; to measure marketing forecasts and programs credibly for non-marketing decision makers; and to assist the majority of business people who need a grounding in common marketing measures.

I have been in marketing in several industries: in the hotel industry (as a marketing executive and as an owner); in consumer products at Nike (for its ACG and Limited Edition businesses); in high-tech enterprise software (at Informix); in my own brand-strategy company called Brand New View; and in university education, at University of Washington, at UC Davis and, currently, at Singapore Management University, where I teach to executives, MBAs and undergraduates. My university teaching has included organizing students into consulting teams to study real companies (more than 60 in the U.S. and Asia) and develop marketing plans for them.

These activities have confirmed my suspicions: marketing is misunderstood. I believe this is because many business people have a narrow and incomplete definition that says marketing is about creating ads, slogans and logos. This misunderstanding is aggravated further by often unrealistically high expectations about what marketing can deliver.

CEOs and CFOs have become preoccupied, almost comically so, with measuring everything in companies today. One can almost imagine them at home after work saying "Honey, what's the ROI on our marriage?", as if they are expecting a call from a Wall Street marriage broker who

1

is impatient for dividends from this merger. While this example is a bit far-fetched, I believe we are close to that point in our companies, with a growing preoccupation to analyze everything. I do not think it is possible to measure everything, nor do I believe it is a good use of time. Some things in life simply happen, despite the best of plans. As the saying goes, "Life is what happens to you while you are busy making other plans." Nevertheless, many marketers have taken this philosophy to an extreme and suggest that marketing really can't be measured. In this context, they struggle to convince colleagues, bosses and subordinates of the merits of their programs and, worse still, the relevance of marketing's role in general. Often this is because they believe their activities are designed for external customers only. Yet when colleagues say they don't understand marketing, the marketers throw up their hands in a dramatic, exasperated, exaggerated fashion, as if to say "Oh come on, what's so hard about this?" The conclusion is inescapable: marketers must market themselves and their programs INSIDE their own companies if they want to earn the ongoing support and funding for their efforts. The challenge for marketers, CEOs and CFOs is knowing what to measure and how to interpret the results (and temper their expectations).

To paraphrase Peter Drucker, *business exists to create a customer and only two functions produce results in this effort: marketing and innovation. All the rest are costs.* The clever marketer will immediately grasp the implications of this remark: marketing produces results.

Marketing academics have published a sizable and growing body of research about marketing metrics and models. Some of these are quite complex, but no less useful for the truly resourceful. In considering the audience for this book, it seemed reasonable to assume that many business people want and need tools that enable them to better understand how marketing contributes to their company's success. If your interest in these tools is stimulated, then I encourage you to do a more extensive review of the marketing research that is available from schools of business, the Marketing Science Institute and the American Marketing Association, among others. While there are many recognized experts in marketing, here are a few I admire whose work is both extensive and relevant to today's marketing practitioners. (This list is by no mean exhaustive. Apologies to those I do not mention but whose work is equally well-regarded.) From this list, I was most influenced by my father, Robert T. Davis, who taught at Stanford for nearly 40 years until his death in 1995. His love of marketing was inspiring and infectious!

- David Aaker
- Roger Best
- Robert T. Davis
- George Day
- John Deighton
- Kevin J. Keller
- Phil Kotler
- Jean-Claude Larreche
- Donald Lehmann
- Theodore Levitt
- David B. Montgomery
- David Reibstein
- Raj Srivistava
- Bernd Schmitt
- J.B. SteenKamp
- Tan Chin Tiong
- Valerie Zeithaml

APPLICABILITY ACROSS CULTURES

I use a mix of actual and hypothetical examples throughout this book. Not all of the Magic Numbers for Consumer Marketing have publicly accessible examples, but the concepts are important; hence the use of hypothetical situations. I introduce a combination of examples from around the world, rather than one region or country, in the hope that you will find them interesting and even refreshing. This creates some minor complications because some marketing concepts, such as market research and brand-name premium, in particular, are useful only to specific regions of the world and, thus, are not universally applicable. Marketing concepts that are useful to companies in the U.S. and Europe may be less appropriate for Asian companies. At the risk of over-simplifying, market and consumer research data is not collected in the same way in many parts of Asia, and Asian companies have different financial reporting requirements as well. In these instances, some of the Magic Numbers will be less relevant.

Of course, Asian companies have their share of business traditions that are not regularly practiced, if even used at all, in the West. In many parts of Asia, the development of deep, almost personal, relationships before transacting business is common. Trust must be established first, and this requires more than a single meeting to accomplish. It can literally take years. But business success is built from the genuine development of these sincere, often complex, relationships. Therefore, while several of the descriptions within the Magic Numbers relating to brand culture and brand equity may seem time-consuming to Western companies, they are powerful catalysts for business development in Asia.

SCOPE OF BOOK

This book is designed to be a quick reference for busy business professionals seeking understandable descriptions of useful marketing measures for consumer marketing. However, I caution you against a rigid adherence to these measures as the "only way" to assess marketing and I will occasionally describe the risks of over-dependence, especially when it excludes the wisdom born of experience and intuition. Non-marketers often expect absolutes, yet marketing is a hybrid: art and science; qualitative and quantitative. There are no perfect formulas or ideal practices that are uniform across or even within industries.

Not every Magic Number described in this book comes with a universally recognized formula. In some cases, there are no specific formulas at all. The book offers a combination of quantitative measures and qualitative frameworks, as both are important to assessing marketing's contribution.

The title, *Magic Numbers for Consumer Marketing*, is a bit intimidating to me. It implies I have special or unique insight into the formulas that measure marketing's performance that have not been discovered before. I do not presume to have such special knowledge. Many of the Magic Numbers will be familiar to you, others less so. But all have been described before (by the aforementioned academics, for example) and applied, for decades in some cases. If there is "Magic" in this book, perhaps it is in bringing together marketing's many concepts for a one-stop easy reference. For that, Nick Wallwork, the publisher, is the magician who deserves credit.

ORGANIZATION OF BOOK

The book has been organized into four broad themes:

- **Market:** Magic Numbers that assess size, share, potential and performance

- **Company:** Magic Numbers that measure general business performance, brand value, and qualitative frameworks that review the organization

- **Customer:** Magic Numbers that analyze customers and customer value

- **Marketing:** Magic Numbers that evaluate marketing programs, including price, marketing communications, and retail performance.

Each Magic Number is described the same way by describing its definition, formula, where the data is found, how to calculate it, what it means in terms of practical impact and potential challenges associated with its use. Specifically, with the quantitative formulas, I will describe what it is and how to use it. With the qualitative frameworks, I will describe how they are structured and what to learn from them.

Part One

MAGIC NUMBERS FOR UNDERSTANDING A MARKET

Understanding the market in which you compete or seek to compete is important only if you want to succeed. If you are a mindless thrill-seeker, then by all means go to market without taking the time to learn anything. While you're at it, don't bother with medical school before becoming a doctor. After all, how hard can neurosurgery be, anyway?

In all seriousness, the risks in misunderstanding the market can be sizable. To be meaningful and relevant, the marketing manager (indeed, the CEO) needs to understand the context in which the company competes. An extreme example: in the late 1990s, high-tech start-ups regularly estimated market potential that was far larger than the actual target market they would ultimately serve. "We're in a $50 billion software market growing 30% per year and only need 1% to be successful" was often the type of "evidence" entrepreneurs supplied. In actuality, the $50 billion software market was really several dozen smaller markets (Enterprise Resource Planning-ERP, Customer Relationship Management-CRM, Sales Force Automation-SFA and so forth), each of which had different levels of financial performance. Therefore, clearly identifying this ensures a company's marketing efforts begin on the right track.

While some of the Magic Numbers may seem quite basic, it is important to work through each, even mentally, to understand how they fit together.

Market Size

THE DEFINITION

Simply put, market size refers to the size of your market. The challenge lies in properly identifying the specific market in which you compete. To clarify, there are a handful of market definitions: a *market* is typically considered the number of existing and potential buyers of your product, or of products in a particular category. Clearly, it would be downright silly to claim all six billion people on earth as your market. There must be a set of characteristics that describe your market if your marketing plans are to have any chance of success. A corollary definition is your *potential market*, which refers to customers in another segment who may ultimately find your products or services attractive, but are also sufficiently different from your primary market that they can be viewed as having unique characteristics as well as common characteristics with the primary market.

THE FORMULA AND ITS COMPONENTS

Determining market size, or "total market", depends on a variety of factors: are you using units to describe your market, or dollars? Are you describing your market size in terms of the total population of possible customers (for example, everyone living in a particular area), or a targeted subset (for example, those living in a specific neighborhood)? Are you evaluating market size based on demographics (age, income, sex…) or psychographics (individual interests, social interests, emotional appeals…)? Knowing which criteria you are using is an important first step, because it provides guidance on subsequent research that you must conduct to properly evaluate the size of your market. Research is important, not just in determining market share, but throughout any market effort, so you might as well get comfortable with it.

In its simplest form, the formula is as follows:

$M_t = C \times Q$

Where

M_t = the total market (in units or dollars)
C = the total number of customers
Q = the average quantity of products customers purchase

Note: I define "average" as the "mean" rather than the "median". The median can be useful if the average appears too vague to be useful. In this instance, the number of responses is ordered from the lowest number of purchases per customer to the highest, with the middle number the "median". This might be useful if it turns out that there is a large variance in quantity purchased such that an average may skew the results too high or too low. For example, if a company surveys its market and gets 10 responses of which seven buy 10 products per year and the other three buy only one, then the median is more useful as it indicates that while the target market size may be smaller (seven versus 10), those who buy frequently are clearly a more appealing target audience. The average would have skewed their number of purchases lower and made the market size estimate smaller.

WHERE'S THE DATA?

Example: Broadly speaking, the global athletic market can be viewed as the aggregate of all the products (footwear, apparel, hard goods) sold by all competitors.

Nike is widely acknowledged as the largest company in the overall global athletic market. In this instance, let's use the footwear product category in the United States. The Sporting Goods Manufacturing Association (SGMA) reported the following statistics about the U.S. athletic footwear market in 2004.

- Consumer spending for athletic footwear rose 3.1% in 2004, to $16.4 billion.

- Total pairs purchased — 492.8 million.

- Average price per pair — $33.18.

- Children's footwear was the fastest-growing segment of the market in consumer spending terms, with over 12% growth in 2004 over 2003, compared to 4.3% for women's and −2.5% for men's.

- Price competition was strongest in men's athletic footwear, where spending declined 1.6% to $7.84 billion and the average price per pair declined 3.7% to $42.12.

- According to consumers, comfort is the most important influence on their purchase of athletic footwear.

- The U.S. market is over four times larger than the Japanese market.

- The running shoe is the #1 category in sales, with nearly 29% of all spending on athletic shoes.

In U.S. market share between 2000 and 2004, Nike's was in the 37–39% range, Reebok's was between 10.9% and 13%, Adidas hovered between 13% and 15.5%, New Balance was between 11% and 12%, and K-Swiss was in the 3–4% range.[1]

However, it is important to clearly define "market size". While Nike is the largest company overall based on the aforementioned criteria, it is not the largest in every product category. Refining the definition of market size from global athletic market to the global soccer shoe market shifts the emphasis from a broad category (all athletic shoes) to a narrower one (soccer shoes). It turns out that Adidas is larger than Nike in sales of global soccer shoes. In 2004, Adidas had $1.15 billion in global sales and 34.5% market share, compared to Nike's nearly $1 billion in soccer sales and 29.8% market share. Further narrowing reveals that, in North America, Adidas had over 50% share to Nike's 34%.[2] However, Nike moved past Adidas in the European soccer market, with 35% market share compared to the 31% of Adidas.[3]

The market size story is different in each of these soccer examples, but it is no less accurate or more misleading to do this — these are simply different ways to define market size (based on regional rather than global markets).

CALCULATING IT

In this example, we know the total units sold and the dollar value of those units. However, we do not know the number of customers. Sure, we know that there are not 492.8 million people living in the U.S., so more than one pair of athletic footwear was purchased per buyer but we do not know how many pairs each customer bought. Nevertheless, market size is a useful formula for assessing its attractiveness.

WHAT IT MEANS AND POTENTIAL CHALLENGES

It is important to be clear about which market you are describing if you want your marketing plans to be meaningful and relevant, as the athletic market examples demonstrate. However, there are still more market size criteria to be considered. For example, when a company wants to launch a new product, it will use market size to gauge the overall market for customers and products in the total market in which it competes. But this is just a first step and smart marketers will want to know more. Knowing the size of the European soccer market would be useful to athletic footwear companies, and the marketing managers would then want to understand several additional factors, including:

- Who are the likely target customers within the market (the European soccer footwear market in this case)?

- How likely are the target customers to purchase your product?

- How many pairs might they purchase?

- What features do they seek in buying soccer shoes?

- Do they support certain brands?

- How important is price in the decision?

- Are there certain stores from which they prefer to buy?

One recommendation to address these questions is to develop a survey featuring these (and more) questions. This can be done in-house, if the company has the marketing research expertise and knowledge of survey design. Otherwise, a market research firm can be hired for this specific issue. The survey can be conducted several ways: in person (in a shopping mall, on the street, at a sports event…), over the phone or via conventional mail (using the company's in-house customer list or a third-party provider list. There will be more on this in Magic Numbers 54 to 60, which describe direct-marketing measures). Each of these methods has strengths and weaknesses. The success of surveying is dependent on the quality of the survey developed — length, type of questions (yes/no versus open), quality of questions — and the method used for conducting it. Responses will often be challenging to summarize because respondents may not answer truthfully, they may try to bias the results (by answering what they think the surveyor would like to hear), or they may simply not know what answer to provide. The challenge for marketers is to decide what the actual market size is based on the information received. If marketers decide that the market size still cannot be determined satisfactorily, then they must decide whether to go forward with the product launch, despite the unsatisfactory information, or to conduct additional research. Additional research may include focus groups (to learn qualitative insights from consumers about specific products) and more sophisticated research that models consumer-choice behavior (conjoint analysis is one well-known tool, among many). Consumer-choice modeling helps you learn about preferences consumers have for one type of product over another, for example. This can be useful in understanding whether a product is likely to be successfully received once it is in the market. However, none of these techniques will guarantee success. To learn more about marketing research and the many tools available, visit www.marketingpower.com (the website for the American Marketing Association) or www.mra-net.org/ (the website for the Marketing Research Association). These are two of the many resources available that can help marketers learn more about marketing research.

Market Size: High-tech

In the mid to late 1990s, the rapid growth of high-tech and, specifically, the start-up software sector, led many entrepreneurs in the industry to make misleading claims about the potential markets in which they competed. Please note that I use the word "misleading" purposely — I do not mean to suggest lies or deceit. Rather, I am suggesting they were simply sloppy in their market size assessments. The reasons, of course, were many, including the mania that existed at the time when it seemed like every high-tech competitor was claiming the size of their market was beyond normal measures of time, space and dimension. Undoubtedly, part of this market sizing was done to articulate the *potential* market, especially to investors. Investors, particularly venture capitalists (VCs), focused their investments into businesses with sizable market opportunities (among several considerations, including the team and the product idea itself). They wanted to see that the market was big enough for the new firm, in addition to the established players. Of course, this led to some ludicrous assessments that sounded somewhat like this:

VC: *"Thanks…that's a great idea. But how large is the market for this overall?"*

Young Entrepreneur: *"It's a 22 gazillion dollar market, growing 200% a day."*

VC: *"Really? Wow. That's impressive. I had no idea the market for toilet paper made from recycled 5 ½ inch floppies was so large. Here's $5 million to get started."*

It's not just high-tech start-ups that fall prey to this type of exaggeration. Even marketing people do this. For some reason, it often appears that a key genetic trait in marketers is the ability to overstate many situations ("This is the biggest product in the history of products"; or, as one marketer told me regarding his product line, "We're #2 in size, but we're a bigger #2 than the #1 company was relative to us". To this day, I have no idea what he meant, but he said it with such enthusiasm I didn't have the heart to question him). When presenting to the CEO, marketers have been known to say that the market size is "HUGE" (actually, marketers sometimes make up words when something is beyond the normal label of "large". Another marketer I knew years ago used to say that market opportunities were "gi-normous"…as in "giant" and "enormous". It was a clever distortion that distracted the executives from the rest of his remarks while they tried to figure out how large "gi-normous" was). Part of the responsibility of a marketer is to assess market size reasonably, not wildly.

[1] Culled from various press releases and articles from SGMA, *BusinessWeek*, *Forbes*, NSGA (National Sporting Goods Association).

[2] SportsScanINFO, a market research firm in West Palm Beach, Florida.

[3] *BusinessWeek*, September 20, 2004.

MAG1C NUM8ER 2

Market Growth

THE DEFINITION

As business people, we hope to be in markets that are growing. If you are in a market that is not growing, you may be in trouble.

THE FORMULA AND ITS COMPONENTS

While market growth is fundamentally a comparison between performance years, the following formula is helpful:

$$G_m = R_I \div R_L$$

Where

G_m = % market growth
R_I = revenue increase this year
R_L = revenues last year

WHERE'S THE DATA?

Developing a clear understanding of market growth is not complex, but it does require more effort than merely scanning the daily paper. It is often helpful to measure your own growth first, for two reasons: first, to see what your growth trend has been the past few years and determine whether your current pace is above or below your recent historical average; and second, to compare your growth to the statistics for competitors in the market. If you are a publicly traded firm, then you can find the information in annual reports. As a private firm, you will have to talk to your accounting and finance team to get the numbers, or at least the overall rate of growth, if you want to compare to the market.

Market data can be easily obtained from industry trade publications, independent market-research firms, product analysts, reputable business magazines, government reports and trade associations.

CALCULATING IT

If the total market revenues were $140 million this year and $100 million last year, the market growth rate is 40% (this was calculated by taking the revenue increase, $40 million, and dividing it by total revenues last year, $100 million).

WHAT IT MEANS AND POTENTIAL CHALLENGES

Market growth merely means the percentage rate (typically on an annual basis) at which the market grew this year compared to last year, or prior years. The unit of measurement is usually either dollars or units. But the strict definition of the terms is less important than what market growth can tell you, or indicate to you. In our example, the market grew 40%. The growth rate can suggest not just growth for one year, but perhaps an important trend. This can be further reinforced by comparing growth rates for the past four or five years. Marketers will want to understand the forces driving this growth. Numerous factors may influence this growth rate: demographic changes, purchase behavior changes, product or market innovations, lower interest rates and so forth are examples of drivers that may describe or influence the growth rate. Once marketers understand the key factors, they can use this information to develop new products, communications campaigns, and price changes to create a competitive advantage for their products. A key challenge, however, is whether the market growth is even relevant to your longer-term strategy.

The thoughtful reader will quickly note that while my example describes market growth, it does not provide a frame of reference. In other words, is a 40% growth rate good or even exceptional, average, or poor? The answer depends on the industry. Furthermore, even within industries there are segments that may perform far differently from others. For example, let's look at some illustrations from the high-tech world. High-tech covers a wide range of products and services, from hardware to software to telecom to bio-tech and more. In software, there are sub-segments in this business as well.

The database software market is generally considered a mature business. In June 2004, the market-intelligence company IDC (A global market intelligence company specializing in information technology and telecommunications markets) reported that the worldwide market for database software declined in 2002, but rebounded slightly in 2003, from $12.6 billion to $13.6 billion, representing a 0.92% growth rate. That is hardly an aggressive growth rate, but compared to retraction the previous year as well as struggles from 2000–2002, this was a positive step. Therefore, for this industry, one might conclude that 0.92% growth, while not exciting, is better than continued decline. At the time of writing, figures for 2004 were not available. However, IDC commented that this pace of growth would continue through 2005, then accelerate in 2006 and 2007, with total revenues reaching $20 billion by 2008. Growing from $13.6 billion to $20 billion is an almost 50% increase, certainly a healthy rate of growth, especially for a market that was struggling mightily in the early 2000s.

However, if one were to look at the business-intelligence software market (software that analyzes data and variables (even in real time), forecasts trends, summarizes results, and delivers information summaries), a very different market growth pattern is revealed. According to IDC, worldwide revenues were $12.5 billion in 2004 and were forecast to grow 7.5% per year for the next several years.

The ECM (enterprise content management; this is software that helps companies manage their internal digital content, among many uses) market will grow to over $9 billion by 2007, a 15% annual growth rate, according to Meta Group (another analyst firm).

Each of these examples reflects the unique conditions and expectations of its specific market. Companies within these individual markets can then compare their own actual and projected growth to analysts' expectations to decide whether their own performance is good or not. Companies in any market would want to know whether their own growth rates are good, bad or indifferent. Researching industry trade publications, global and regional trends and even watching competitors will help you better understand your own performance and whether it is a cause for celebration or concern. If you are in the hotel business, then learning more about your own industry trends would be key to deciding if you are performing satisfactorily. Even within the hotel industry there is a wide range of sub-markets, including (but not limited to) budget, mid-range, luxury, long-term stay, conference centers and resorts. Of course, knowing your geographic trends helps as well since, for example, a luxury hotel in Tokyo with 65% occupancy may seem good, unless other luxury hotels are running 80% occupancies in that same market. The same is true for every industry and market. To understand market growth in your business, you need to do some homework to determine if your performance compares favorably or whether you ought to think about switching careers.

Gateway and Dell

Let's look at company-specific examples. Your market may be growing very rapidly, such as the PC market experienced in the 1990s. But it is relatively meaningless if you neglect other factors such as pricing trends. Gateway Computer faced this very issue in competition with Dell. In 1996, both companies had approximately $5 billion in sales. Dell had a larger market share in the direct-to-customer PC market, but Gateway was a respectable #2. By 1998, Dell had grown to $12.3 billion, while Gateway had grown to $7.5 billion. Part of the reason for this may be that, in 1996, Gateway chose to pursue the consumer segment in its marketing efforts, in the hope of gaining market share with millions of consumers. It built expensive showcase retail stores (that carried no inventory), attempting to differentiate itself further from Dell. But prices in the PC market were declining as the industry commoditized and Gateway found itself struggling to add value (and margin) to this increasingly low-price business. In the meantime, Dell focused its energy on the large business segment that often demanded PCs and numerous add-on (high margin) services. In effect, Dell was able to leverage a single large business customer into a sale of thousands of computers and associated services, increasing its units in the marketplace. These two approaches highlight that a focus on market share by itself is only one aspect of marketing strategy. Clearly, in retrospect, Gateway's choice handicapped its revenue growth while Dell's efforts accelerated its revenue growth. Gateway's market share continued to decline through early 2004 (sales relative to Dell).

However, be aware that to measure growth (and, indeed, market share and market penetration, as we shall see), you must be quite clear about what it is you are measuring. Is it growth of total market revenues? Or growth of total market dollars available for purchasing? Or is it the rate at which new customers are being acquired? Or the rate at which the three most significant competitors are growing? Knowing the whether frame of reference will help you understand your market growth rate is better, worse or similar to other companies in your industry.

MAG1C NUM8ER

3

Market Coverage

There are two approaches for market coverage that are both relevant and useful for marketers.

Approach 1

THE DEFINITION

There are three strategies that a marketer can choose in determining how best to increase market coverage:

- Concentrated marketing:

This describes a company's efforts to attract consumers in a niche or small segment of the market. As the term implies, firms concentrate their resources on reaching this audience in the hope of gaining a large and even dominant share of this niche market.

- Differentiated marketing:

This strategy directs a firm to create several different marketing programs, each targeted to a specific segment, with unique promotional offers, product feature variation and service options.

- Undifferentiated marketing:

Here, a company uses a single marketing campaign to cover all segments in the market. Similarly, this strategy can also be accomplished by offering one product for the entire market.

Approach 2

THE DEFINITION[1]

Coverage can be understood and described in terms of particular combinations of products and segments, based on a firm's allocation of products to specific segments in which it wishes to compete. The matrices at the end of the section outline five different possibilities:

Single-segment concentration: a company utilizing this will focus its product and marketing efforts on one segment. Firms with limited resources often find this approach to be most effective since it minimizes the risk of the company spreading its product and marketing dollars across too many product and market needs. Start-ups in the introductory phase of their life-cycle would find this approach particularly useful since they simply do not have the resources to reach multiple markets simultaneously until they hit the growth phase later on. Alternatively, firms specializing in a very specific area, such as bio-tech solutions for various cancers, may also choose this since they do not need nor care about reaching non-cancer segments.

Product specialization: In this situation, you concentrate on a particular product, but market it to many segments. If you are adept at this, then you will build a reputation for expertise in this area. An example of this is Pixar, which has developed a reputation for top-quality films using very specific computer animation. Its films appeal to a wide range of market segments, from kids to adults, and even across cultures. It doesn't make washing machines, food or nose-hair trimmers. It simply concentrates on computer-animated films.

Market specialization: Market specialization is concerned with offering multiple products to specific customers (unlike a specific product to multiple customers as we saw in product specialization) who have particular needs or interest. LVMH (the French luxury-goods giant discussed later in the book) provides an example of this. It does not spend time, money or product development efforts trying to reach budget consumers. Its area of expertise is consumers who love and appreciate luxury products and LVMH offers over 50 well-known luxury brands (Louis Vuitton, Givenchy, Krug, Donna Karan, Christian Dior, to name a few).

Selective specialization: Firms focusing here provide more products to more market segments. This is where your marketing can get a bit tricky because the line between markets in which you choose to concentrate and products you decide to offer can quickly escalate from controlled selectivity to uncontrolled chaos that spreads your marketing investments too thin. It is tempting for rapidly growing companies to expand into new markets quickly and to diversify their product offerings, both to appeal to markets and to spread risk. A company that does this well is Mars, a privately-owned, U.S.-based firm, best known for its snack foods, including Mars Bars (Milky Way in the U.S.), Snickers and M&Ms. Mars also competes successfully in pet care, main-meal foods and in branded beverages. Perhaps most interestingly, Mars has an electronics business. At first glance, you might think electronics is unrelated to the company's other businesses. Yet the company pioneered electronic automated payments in vending machines that dispense food (as well as public telephones and ticket machines for mass-transit systems). These businesses comprise the extent of Mars' selective specialization. Unlike Procter & Gamble, Mars is not in dozens of different consumer-products categories. And unlike many electronics firms, it is not manufacturing a wide range of consumer electronics. In each instance, Mars is a market leader in a specialized area.

Full-market coverage: In this area, companies attempt to serve all customers with multiple products. Arguably, Toyota and General Motors both try to provide full-market coverage, offering automobiles from entry-level to luxury consumers. (For General Motors, this ranges from the low-end Saturn and Chevrolet to the high-end Cadillac. For Toyota, this span of coverage includes the Echo at the entry level and Lexus at the luxury level.) General Motors has not done nearly as well with this strategy in recent decades as Toyota. Clearly, firms attempting such an approach must have substantial resources to even have a chance at success. On the other hand, if you are lacking in resources and simply wish to take your company on a sleighride to hell, then by all means attempt full-market coverage. Full-market coverage is similar to those restaurants we've all seen that offer dozens of menu items from a variety of cultures and countries. "Wow," you say to yourself. "What a great selection! How do they do it?" The reality is often that the selection looks great, but the quality is disappointing. Be prepared to invest heavily for years to make this work.

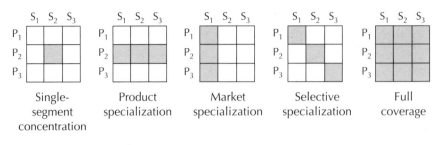

(S = segments, P = products)

THE FORMULA

There is no formula, as coverage is a set of strategic choices and/or options. Your choice of coverage strategy can be evaluated using other Magic Numbers (customer-acquisition analysis, market-share measures, brand measures, for example) to determine its attractiveness. Furthermore, a company should select a market-coverage strategy with a keen eye on its own skills and competencies (see Magic Number 24, Brand-Culture Framework, for more insight on how companies can do this).

WHERE'S THE DATA?

Information on coverage is dependent on the strategy chosen. Much of the information for these strategies, however, can be found in a wide range of sources, including market research firms, financial or product analyst reports, strategic consultancies and industry publications, trade associations and similar vertical media.

It is important to use more than one source whenever embarking on a study to understand your market(s) better. Each source may employ a different research methodology, including subtle differences in survey questions for example, that yield widely different results. It cannot be overstated that your choice of strategy is pivotal to acquiring (through original or third-party research), understanding and using the highest quality and most reliable data.

CALCULATING IT

"Calculating" is not the best term to use here since calculation implies a formula, and market coverage does not lend itself to a formula. Therefore, a more accurate term would be "determining", since you are effectively deciding which of the market-coverage approaches best fits for your organization. This, too, depends on your choice of strategy, as that then influences your assumptions and, ultimately, the measures you select to evaluate your options. For example, if you are trying to determine a market-coverage strategy for x-ray glasses, you should know what the total market is (see Magic Numbers 1 and 2), determine the segment(s) you are targeting (in this case, perhaps the target audience comprises people who like to see through buildings), describe the characteristics consumers with this interest have in common, try to understand what the differences are for consumers who like x-ray glasses but do not share other characteristics (to see if different marketing communication strategies with unique appeals are a better approach to reaching these audiences), evaluate the number and location of the various distribution points (stores, for example) through which your products would be sold and enumerate how many products you sell to that segment compared to how many the competitors sell. This will give you a general sense of your market for x-ray glasses and it will also refine the market picture so that you can choose the appropriate strategy.

Keep in mind that market coverage actually encompasses an understanding of what the current market is as well as the potential market. If you are trying to determine your *potential* market, then you would still want to understand the total market and specific segments, but you would also want to clearly understand those customers who are currently not buying your products but are within your ability to convert to being your customers. This will tell you of your potential coverage. You can then compare potential coverage to actual coverage to gain a strong sense of the strategic opportunities (and challenges) ahead of you.

WHAT IT MEANS AND POTENTIAL CHALLENGES

As you will have gathered, clearly defining "coverage" gets a bit tricky because of the different strategies available and the concomitant research needed to understand the efficacy of each strategy. Also, market coverage is a slippery concept and, to the uninitiated, can often mean similar things to market size and even market share.

Nike ACG (All Conditions Gear)

Nike's ACG business develops footwear, apparel and accessory products for outdoor sports enthusiasts. As defined in the athletic industry, outdoor sports include activities like rock climbing, cycling, mountain biking, hiking, kayaking, windsurfing and skate boarding. When I was the product marketing manager for ACG, the business was in transition. For years prior, ACG's products had been distributed to the market using Nike's in-line sales force, meaning the sales reps who sold the majority of the company's products (tennis, basketball, running…). This undifferentiated approach proved to be ineffective in growing the outdoor business because the profile of the outdoor consumer turned out to be quite different from that of the typical sports consumer. Traditional sports consumers generally enjoyed team activities and had been educated over the years to purchase their products at typical sporting goods stores. But outdoor consumers prided themselves on their independence, their ability to take on and overcome extreme challenges (rock climbing without ropes, for example) and did NOT see themselves as being remotely similar to the traditional sports consumer. Consequently, they rarely if ever frequented typical sporting goods stores because they did not perceive them as credible or authentic providers of outdoor sports. Psychologically, the outdoor consumers did not see themselves as sharing any of the same values as the traditional sports consumer.

Traveling with the ACG product team to different outdoor sports events, including "fat tire" events (mountain bike races), rock climbing, and windsurfing competitions, shed new light (particularly to me) on the different expectations these customers had for products. Furthermore, these customers were quite blunt in their belief that Nike did not understand them, as evidenced by Nike's distribution through traditional sporting goods channels. We took video cameras with us to tape consumer feedback and show them in their environment, and to bring this visual information back to Nike to show at product meetings. This helped change Nike's perceptions of these consumers and suggested that a more differentiated coverage strategy was required if Nike wanted to maximize its potential with this market. In fact, a differentiated approach was only part of it as it was also important to *concentrate* on these customers through highly targeted communication programs and highly differentiated product offerings.

We revamped the product line by incorporating designs and technologies that were relevant to the outdoor consumer and moved away from Nike's previous practice of modifying "in-line" silhouettes and repackaging them for this market. The ACG team recruited an independent sales force that was deeply familiar with and dedicated to the outdoor market. These reps were also connected to outdoor retailers, which facilitated Nike expanding its distribution base to these retailers specifically. Over 18 months, this combination of differentiated and concentrated strategies proved to be a successful approach and the ACG business grew by more than 100%. The ACG business vaulted to #1 in the outdoor market in terms of total units and revenues, from the #5 position previously. Of course, it helped that the general consumer marketplace was expanding its interest and, consequently, was seeking products beyond traditional sports products.

Successful strategies, in hindsight, are often the result of dedicated strategic choices that are in concert with emerging trends. It goes without saying that the success of ACG at Nike was not, nor could it have been, entirely foreseen. But the resulting success would likely have been diminished had we not spent time and effort to develop strategies tailored more specifically to the needs of the outdoor consumer, irrespective of the coincident, and fortunately timed, trend of the broader market's increased interested in outdoor products.

[1] Abell, Derek F. (1980), *Defining the Business: The Starting Point of Strategic Planning*, Prentice Hall, Chap. 8, pp.192–196.

MAGIC NUMBER 4

Market Share

THE DEFINITION

Market share is your sales as a percentage of total sales of all companies in your product market.

THE FORMULA AND ITS COMPONENTS

$$M_s = \frac{S}{M_t}$$

Where

M_s = market share, expressed in percentage terms
S = sales
M_t = total market

WHERE'S THE DATA?

Sales figures for your company should be with your accounting or finance office. Sales figures for the competitors in your product market can be found in their annual reports if they are publicly traded, or possibly in industry trade publications or market research reports. It should be relatively easy to gather the appropriate information from a simple review of your own sales as compared to the sales of the total market for products of your type.

CALCULATING IT

For example, if you sell $15 million of products in a total market of $150 million, then your market share is 10%.

$$\frac{\$15,000,000}{\$150,000,000} = 10\%$$

Coke and Pepsi

Of course, market share can be specific to lines of business or individual products. When comparing Coke to Pepsi, for example, one must be careful to ensure the right comparison is being made. Let's look at the U.S. market, for example. Both companies have diversified businesses, including alternative non-cola beverages and, in Pepsi's case, snack foods. Therefore, saying Coke's market share is larger than Pepsi's may be true in the cola market (where Coke had a dominant 44% share of market in 2003), but not necessarily true when considering the aggregate of their respective combined businesses. Pepsi's non-cola beverage business is larger than Coke's, for example.[1] When defined as a percentage of the total U.S. beverage business, Pepsi led Coke 28% to 27% in overall beverage sales in 2003. Furthermore, market share can be applied to channels within an overall market, as in the case of Pepsi and Coke's respective efforts in retail versus fast-food distribution. Nevertheless, the overall concept is the same.

WHAT IT MEANS AND POTENTIAL CHALLENGES

Market share describes the percentage of the total market represented by your company's products. It is a useful marketing metric as it is an indication of your company's penetration relative to the competition. However, market share is only one of several guides for assessing your success. It is not sufficient just to celebrate market-share gains beyond your plan; you must also analyze how you achieved these gains. Did you cut price? If so, then your company margins are affected. Did a competitor stumble? If so, then maybe you're next. In other words, don't rely solely on market share without understanding the context in which it occurred.

Apple Computer

For example, if you have 2% market share of a 175 million-unit personal computer market such as Apple did in 2003, then you have a sizable 3.5 million-unit business. Of course, the rest of the world's computers run on the Microsoft platform, which is a veritable Jupiter compared to your grain of space dust, so a 2% share is relatively meaningless, except to say you are unlikely to overtake Microsoft anytime before the next big bang. On the other hand, if you have 2% share in a highly fragmented market, where the largest competitor has 5%, then you at least have hope of one day becoming leader and can develop strategies accordingly. In sum, market share can tell you how much of the market your sales represent relative to the total of all competitors in the same product market.

MARKET SIZE AND MARKET SHARE

These two measures go together. But, for these to have any real meaning, several simple, yet often overlooked, steps need to be completed. First, you must determine what units will be used to measure your sales: dollars, pairs, dollops, …whatever. Just be sure to use the same measure throughout your analysis. Second, you have to do some investigation to understand your market. This used to be called "Market Research", although it is increasingly termed "Business Intelligence" (no, this is not an oxymoron). Business-intelligence gathering will reveal information about your overall market that can then be used to describe target markets (i.e. specific customer types), define product offerings and develop marketing communications that capture the imagination of the customers. Once you get the hang of doing this, using market size and market share together will be as easy as breathing.

Market size and market share may be simple to understand, but they reveal important insights about the performance of your business and your products as well as the overall market.

Nike ACG (again)

As mentioned earlier, unit market share is merely market share expressed in units sold (pairs of shoes, in Nike's case) relative to total units sold by all competitors in the market. We were less concerned with market share expressed in dollars. The basic reason was that we wanted our shoes on as many feet as possible. But our team also knew that Nike had specific internal profitability standards every product had to meet. If the product did not meet those standards, it did not stay in the market long or did not even get to market. Defining market-share goals in terms of units provided a very practical guide for competitive strategy (it forced us to look at the four competitors above us and understand their market performance), target market selection (to expand our share of the outdoor customer, we had to understand them better, translate that understanding into products they could appreciate, which would then allow us to more credibly sell more pairs to them), distribution (selecting channels that would allow us to reach the target audience most effectively), pricing (at higher prices we wouldn't be able to reach our market share goals, at lower prices, we wouldn't achieve our internal profitability goals), materials selection (to sell many pairs at a reasonable price, we couldn't make our shoes out of titanium), and marketing communications (knowing we had to gain a certain number and type of customers told us how we could best tailor a message that was appealing and which media vehicles connected us most effectively with our target customers). We eventually achieved our goal of becoming #1.

[1] Carlotti Jr., Stephen J.; Coe, Mary Ellen; Perrey, Jesko, "Making Brand Portfolios Work", *McKinsey Quarterly* 2004 Number 4, p.28.

Market Penetration

THE DEFINITION

This is a comparison of a market's current market demand vis-à-vis its potential market demand. Market penetration serves as a useful guide for opportunities for all companies in the market.

THE FORMULA AND ITS COMPONENTS

$$M_P = \frac{D_c}{D_p}$$

Where

M_P = Market penetration
D_c = Current market demand
D_p = Potential market demand

Current market demand describes the total number of products that could be purchased by a pre-defined target-customer group in a specific market area under specific business conditions and marketing programs for all firms in the market.

Potential market demand describes the *added* opportunities available to the same companies for the same products under the same conditions. As you might surmise, potential market demand is influenced by type of product, pricing, new marketing appeals and a host of other factors. Some products lend themselves to added potential, such as many consumer non-durables (food, beverage and grocery products, for example), while other products have less added potential, such as a sports or entertainment event. This is due partly to the types of products (when popular grocery items are discounted, for instance, it often drives temporary demand and increases the total dollars in the market than would otherwise have "naturally" been spent). Sports and entertainment events have a narrower appeal (everyone needs food, not everyone needs to see a professional soccer match) and limited live seating. Additional marketing spent on them will generate increased costs per remaining seat.

WHERE'S THE DATA?

See Magic Numbers 1–6.

CALCULATING IT

Let's assume we are analyzing the market for pizza in a selected city. Current demand indicates a market valued at $8 million annually. However, past industry marketing efforts indicate that price promotions boost business by 25%. Therefore,

$$M_P = \frac{\$8,000,000}{\$10,000,000}$$

This indicates a market penetration of 80%, which is quite high and also suggests that acquiring the remaining customers becomes increasingly expensive on a per-customer basis as the same marketing investment is spread among a smaller number of people. However, let's say that price promotions actually increase business 75%.

$$M_P = \frac{\$8,000,000}{\$14,000,000}$$

Market penetration is now 57%, which can indicate that there is more room for all pizza companies in the market to increase their growth potential. Obviously, the lower the market penetration number, the higher the potential for all firms to increase growth.

WHAT IT MEANS AND POTENTIAL CHALLENGES

As simple as the calculation is, there are challenges. First, market potential implies the cooperation of all firms in the market to test price promotions simultaneously, which is not likely to happen since they are also competing against each other and will look for additional market programs to make their pizza more attractive vis-à-vis their competitors. Second, not all competitor products are the same. In the case of pizza, different crust, sauce and even cheese combinations can result in a different-tasting pizza, so a price promotion will not necessarily stimulate a corresponding increase in demand. This would be true of other food and beverage items and, to a lesser extent, other select grocery items. Third, while past marketing programs (such as lowering prices, in this case) indicated increased response, there is no guarantee that consumers will respond similarly in the future. Marketing is a balancing act of perpetual fine-tuning based on market response.

Nevertheless, as an indicator of opportunities, market penetration can be a useful starting point to testing various programs and seeing which offer the most significant, positive responses.

Market-Share Index

THE DEFINITION

This is a close cousin of market share but it includes variables that affect the consumer's eventual purchase decision and, therefore, can exert additional influence on your company's final market share. By understanding each variable better, your company can choose whether and where to concentrate more resources to improve market-share performance.

THE FORMULA AND ITS COMPONENTS[1]

$$M_{si} = P_a \times P_p \times B_i \times A \times P_{pur}$$

Where

M_{si} = market-share index

P_a = product awareness (the number of people aware of your product in your target market compared to the overall population in the target market)

P_p = product preference (is the product and/or its features attractive?)

B_i = intention to buy (is the product's price attractive?)

A = availability of product (can the product be found in the marketplace?)

P_{pur} = product purchase (is buying the product a positive experience?)

WHERE'S THE DATA?

Collecting the data for this analysis is tricky, but not impossible. It implies that you undertake some basic market research to determine each of the formula's components. Each component can be determined from surveys and/or predictive modeling techniques with the exception of product preference and availability of product. Product preference can be calculated using several techniques including *conjoint analysis*. Conjoint analysis is used for measuring several key business and customer areas, including the value of brand names compared to competitors; how customers react to different pricing levels; the impact of new products introduced by competitors; customer response to different advertising messages; different combinations of features, and more. It helps marketers understand how customers make trade-offs with a product's benefits, attributes or features. It can be fairly complex, but there are software packages available that allow companies to conduct a conjoint analysis.

Availability of product is determined through an analysis of your own distribution, by asking such questions as:

- Is the product available and easy to buy?

- What is the number of actual distribution points compared to the total number of distribution points, which provides a percentage of share or penetration?

CALCULATING IT

Let's assume that our data gathering reveals the following statistics:

- P_a = Product awareness = 52% (48% are unaware)

- P_p = Product preference = 76% (24% find it unattractive)

- B_i = Intention to buy = 55% (45% do not intend to buy)

- A = Availability of product = 40% (60% product not available)

- P_{pur} = Product purchase = 38% (62% had a disappointing purchase experience)

$$M_{pen} = P_a \times P_p \times B_i \times A \times P_{pur}$$
$$M_{pen} = .52 \times .76 \times .55 \times .40 \times .38$$
$$= .033$$
$$= 3.3\%$$

WHAT IT MEANS AND POTENTIAL CHALLENGES

This analysis can be helpful for a number of reasons. It can indicate where you may have problems in your "go to market" efforts so that you can focus on those areas that can help you improve penetration. For example, in the above analysis, 76% of the people who are aware of your product prefer it, which is a reasonably strong level of preference for the product. Interestingly, only 52% of the market is aware of the product. Therefore, the company can focus its marketing efforts on communications to increase awareness. If, through these efforts, the company succeeds in increasing awareness to 75%, then the M_P increases from 3.3% to 4.7%. In this example, another area of improvement is in the buying experience. Only 38% of the buyers had a good buying experience. Therefore, the company could undertake a point-of-sale training program that teaches sales people on the floor how to improve service with a view to enhancing customers' purchasing experience. Let's assume the company is able to flip these numbers through just such a training program, so that 62% of the buyers report a positive buying experience. Keeping the aforementioned increase in awareness level and now factoring in the improved buying experience level yields a market penetration of 7.7%.

Be aware that each component does have its own challenges. Product awareness will tell you the percentage of customers in your target market that are aware of your product (you could measure the percentage of people overall in the market that are aware of your product, but it would be less meaningful because this would presume that all people in the market may have an interest in the product if they were only aware of it). If awareness is low, then it indicates you have potential to increase awareness. The corollary is that it will cost money to increase awareness since you will have to invest in advertising, sales, promotions and other marketing communications efforts. It will also cost money to improve the buyer's satisfaction at the time of purchase. But if your goal is to improve your penetration and beat your competition, then these are worthy of serious consideration.

This provides companies with a guide on whether there remains significant potential or not in their markets. Generally, a lower penetration share signals that the company has additional (and hopefully, achievable) share it can capture.

Nike Ekins

Nike is well known for its marketing prowess. The company approaches its efforts from several standpoints. The common misperception is that Nike throws a great deal of money into two areas: television advertising and athlete endorsements. While these areas figure prominently in Nike's efforts, they are just two of a multitude of levers available to the company. Nike believes strongly in its point-of-sale efforts because it invests a great deal into making the highest-quality products that can perform in rigorous athletic efforts. The company wants customers to understand what makes its product designs unique and why its technology is central to the user's enjoyment of the product and the sport they are playing. A key component of Nike's strategy is a team of people known as "Ekins" (singular, it is "Nike" spelled backwards). The Ekins are responsible for visiting every retail account where Nike products are distributed and giving clinics to retail customer-service staff about the technologies and materials that are used in each product and why they are important to the end customers. Doing this helps Nike gain an edge in the market because it

- demonstrates to the retailer that it cares about helping the retailer succeed

- creates expectation in each store for the next product launches, knowing that Nike will come to explain the products, the technology, the market trends

- helps Nike become one of the first, if not the first, brands recommended when customers seek athletic products because the retail staff (who work for the retailer and not for Nike) have been educated by Nike

- helps explain the purpose for each design and the different types of customers who would benefit.

The end result, hopefully, is that customers end up with a more enjoyable buying experience because they have received great service that is thoughtful to their needs.

[1] Best, Roger J., *Market-Based Management: Strategies for Growing Customer Value and Profitability*, pp.86–87, Pearson Education, ©2005, 2004, 2000, 1997.

Additional information on this subject can be found in Kotler, Philip; Ang Swee Hoon; Leong Siew Meng; and Tan Chin Tiong, *Marketing Management: An Asian Perspective*, p.137, Prentice Hall, ©2003.

Market–Share Potential

THE DEFINITION

This refers to a firm's potential *share* in the total potential *market*.

THE FORMULA AND ITS COMPONENTS

Market-share potential provides targets for an ideal or hoped-for response, based on the factors described in the market-share index. Overall, the same formula applies as in market-share index, but companies set targets for improvements in each of the market-share index factors to determine their own market-share potential.

WHERE'S THE DATA?

See Magic Numbers 1–6 for baseline data. Companies should then establish targets based on realistic *stretch* goals or criteria.

CALCULATING IT

The following chart[1] illustrates how to calculate market-share potential. The potential response factors reflect a company's goals or preferred end-state. They are both achievable but challenging, providing ambitious targets that, if achieved, lead to a sizable increase in the company's market-share index. While this illustration is hypothetical, you can see the potential this company would have if it were to improve its various market-share factors. Individually, these factors become areas of focus around which employees can design programs that push the firm to an improved performance. Collectively, these factors can lead to a far more effective company performance in the market.

Market-Share Factors	Where the company is ↓ Current Response	What the company wants ↓ Potential Response	Size of gap ↓ Difference
Product awareness	.52	.75	.23
Product preference	.76	.80	.04
Intention to buy	.55	.75	.20
Availability of product	.40	.70	.30
Product purchase	.38	.80	.42
Market-Share Index	.033	.252	.219

WHAT IT MEANS AND POTENTIAL CHALLENGES

It is apparent that improvements in each market-share factor can lead to demonstrable performance improvements for the company overall, reflected in a substantially higher market-share index potential. More importantly, by improving each of these factors, a company is setting two competitive challenges:

- First, a higher entry barrier, because new firms have numerous factors on which they need to concentrate and even excel if they are to succeed in a new market;

- Second, a higher competitive barrier for existing firms, because if a company is successful at establishing this enhanced performance level, then a competitor has multiple activities it needs to improve, not just one, in order to remain competitive. As we shall see later, it is far harder to copy a company and its behaviors than it is a product. And these behaviors, factors in this case, are what truly set strong performers apart from and ahead of also-rans.

The challenges, of course, are that as a company embarks on an improvement campaign for each of these factors, competitors are unlikely to sit idly by while another firm begins to eclipse them, unless that competitor is distracted by bad management and/or internal problems. Assuming the competitors are reasonably well-run businesses, then they will be alert to another company's efforts and find ways either to match or exceed these by focusing on their own respective market-share factors. Of course, the good news for consumers is that if more companies in a given industry compete on this basis, then the consumers are bound to benefit from improved products, service, availability and so forth, which is healthy for the economy overall.

[1] Best, Roger J., *Market-Based Management*, Pearson Prentice Hall ©2004, p.88.

MAGIC
NUM8ER

8

Market–Share Development Performance

THE DEFINITION

This refers to the effectiveness of a company's efforts by calculating the ratio of its actual market-share to its potential market-share.

THE FORMULA AND ITS COMPONENTS

$$M_{sd} = \frac{M_a}{M_p}$$

Where

M_{sd} = market-share development
M_a = actual market-share
M_p = potential market-share

WHERE'S THE DATA?

As with Magic Numbers 1–6, the necessary data is found in industry research, trade journals, your own calculations and research, or third-party research.

CALCULATING IT

Using the figures from the market-share index and market-share potential, we can now calculate the market-share development performance:

$$M_{sd} = \frac{.033}{.252}$$
$$= .13$$
$$= 13\%$$

This 13% figure says that the company reached 13% of its potential in its efforts to build market-share. It stands to reason that there is substantial room to improve on this. Understanding the opportunity becomes even more obvious when the market-share development performance is combined with the market penetration.

Roger J. Best, Emeritus Professor of Marketing at University of Oregon, suggests that graphing these results on a simple matrix can assist companies to determine their strategic options. Let's take a look:

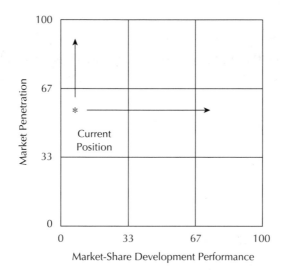

As you review this chart, you will notice that this company can create additional value by improving its performance in either or both dimensions. Depending on its emphasis, this company can develop strategic options that take advantage of the opportunities. Market-penetration improvements will help develop the overall market further if more firms in the industry work toward attracting customers through a combination of marketing programs. In effect, this rising tide of marketing investment would "lift all boats". Market-share development performance improvements will help the company improve its own market development. It may be a bit of a simplification, but this chart demonstrates that if companies competing in a common industry work toward improving their own market development, then the industry as a whole benefits.

MAGIC NUMBER 9

Market Demand

THE DEFINITION

This refers to the demand for product based on new customers to the market and existing customers who already buy the product.

THE FORMULA AND ITS COMPONENTS

$$M_d = P_r + P_n$$

Where

M_d = market demand
P_r = repeat or replacement purchases (existing customers)
P_n = new purchases

WHERE'S THE DATA?

Market data for demand, repeat purchases and new purchases can be found in industry trade journals, industry research reports, general business magazines with special issues devoted to different industry sectors and your own research into market trends.

CALCULATING IT

One of the hottest products right now is the portable music player. Within this market are players that incorporate the latest technology (the other market mainly comprises players that use a hard drive). This segment of the market is expected to grow 45% annually for the next six years,[1] from more than 20 million units in 2004 to 194 million units by 2010, by which time, too, the total portable music-player market is forecast to reach $58 billion. Statistics on replacement and repurchase rates are still incomplete, given the relative infancy of this market (especially with the emergence of Apple's iPod in 2001), so for the purposes of this exercise we will assume that existing customers of the technologically advanced players will repurchase or replace their equipment every one to two years.

Looking at the growth statistics for such players using straight-line approximation, the numbers of units sold look like this (in millions of units):

2004	2005	2006	2007	2008	2009	2010
20	30	43	62	90	134	194

Market demand in 2005 is 31.3 million units. Since customers will repurchase or replace their players every one to two years, we can assume that the majority of those purchased in each year will be replaced the following year. Since we don't know precisely what this figure is, we'll assume that 17.2 million are replacement purchases from existing customers (the average of the total demand for the first two years). Therefore, the remaining 14.1 million units are new purchases.

$$M_d = P_r + P_n$$
$$M_d = 17.2 \text{ million} + 14.1 \text{ million}$$
$$= 31.3 \text{ million units}$$

As mentioned earlier, reliable statistics for the high-tech portable music-player market are still emerging, but it is reasonable to assume that the level of replacement purchase will increase, while the level of new purchases will decrease (since it will be harder and harder to find new customers). At some point, it will be possible to forecast what the "ultimate" market demand might be a few years down the road when the market has reached its peak. At that time, the challenge for companies will be deciding whether to compete on the commodity basis, as many of the players are doing right now, or the specialty basis, as Apple's iPod does.

[1] Source: "Digital Audio Players Set to Explode", Informa Media Group, Press Release 21 July 2004. http://www.telecoms.com/marlin/30000000461/ARTICLEVIEW/mp_articleid/20017286541/mp_pubcode/IMG_press?welcome=true&proceed=true&MarEntityId=1113415110463&entHash=102b352cb95&UType=true

MAG1C NUM8ER

10 Future Demand

THE DEFINITION

This is an estimate of the future demand from consumers for your products.

THE FORMULA AND ITS COMPONENTS

The basic formula is composed of two parts: company demand and market demand, as follows:

Company demand $= D = M_s \times M_{td}$

Where

M_s = market share
M_{td} = total market demand

Total market demand (TMD) $= B \times Q \times P$

Where

B = the number of buyers for your product in the market
Q = the average quantity purchased
P = the average unit price (retail)

Before you calculate these basic components, you need to take a few preliminary market research steps to get a better understanding of the situation in your market:

- estimate general economic conditions, including consumer-spending patterns, inflation and interest rates, and employment statistics.

- describe the business trends in your sector and create a business forecast — business investment patterns, and capital flows from the various capital-market suppliers (banks, venture capitalists, funds).

- develop a company-specific forecast on sales, profitability, market share, and contribution per unit.

Doing this preparatory work does not have to be life-consuming, but it does need to be done to facilitate a more accurate future demand forecast.

WHERE'S THE DATA?

Most of the general economic data can be found in business publications, government budget offices and economic journals. Even a cursory search of the web will provide information in these topics. The data for your industry, particularly the capital information, will be found in several sources. Financial industry analysts, brokerage houses, venture-capital associations and banking reports, among others, will provide regularly updated data on these facts. The company-specific figures will most likely be found in your finance and accounting departments or, if you have a robust marketing group, your marketing research department. Furthermore, if your company is publicly traded, then you will be able to glean some of this information from the annual reports. Assuming your marketing department is up to standard, then it should have the latest market share information, and the sales department ought to have reliable figures on recent sales and the demand pipeline.

CALCULATING IT

I will use a hypothetical example to illustrate. Ming has taken over as the product line manager for a new wallet made from recycled toothpaste tubes (it's called the "Squeezer"). The wallet has the virtue of being flexible and your money smells like peppermint when you pull it out. The Squeezer retails for $20. Market research has led her to the conclusion that the market for the Squeezer is close to 35 million people. Because of its unique materials and specialty position, the Squeezer has gained a market share of 20% in the otherwise fragmented, commodity-driven wallet market. Market demand will be calculated first, since it directly influences company demand.

The following assumptions describe the wallet market:

- The average customer buys two wallets per year.

- The average unit price is $20 (the same as the Squeezer).

- There are 35 million buyers in this market.

- The Squeezer has 20% market-share.

Plugging these figures into the TMD formula yields the following:

$M_{td} = B \times Q \times P$
$M_{td} = 35,000,000 \times 2 \times 20 = \$1,400,000,000$

Now that's a big market demand! The rest of the calculation for future demand is as follows:

Company demand $= D = M_s \times M_{td}$

$D = 20\% \times \$1,400,000,000 = \$280,000,000$

Therefore, future demand based on current sales price and current market share is $280,000,000. Not bad.

WHAT IT MEANS AND POTENTIAL CHALLENGES

But remember, future demand is another Magic Number that is only as good as the research you put in to understand the economy, your industry and your own company's metrics. Even with perfect information (which you will never have), you have to realize that the data you are using is historical. Much like the proverbial "random walk" description of stock investing, which suggests that a stock's past performance is not indicative of its future movement,* your efforts to predict future demand for your products based on the past will not be accurate. However, they may not be far off, either. But don't beat your head against a wall or fire your marketing team just because the numbers don't end up being the same as the forecast. After all, if you really COULD predict the future accurately, you wouldn't be reading this book, would you?

*First introduced by Burton Malkiel in 1973 in his book, *A Random Walk Down Wall Street*.

Part Two

MAGIC NUMBERS FOR
UNDERSTANDING YOUR COMPANY

MAGIC NUMBERS FOR UNDERSTANDING YOUR COMPANY

This next set of Magic Numbers for Consumer Marketing takes us from understanding the market overall as described in Part One, to understanding the company overall. Key financial measures used in a marketing context are described. Furthermore, brand as a strategic concept is introduced. A key aspect to brand strategy is measuring the factors that comprise brand value. There are numerous qualitative frameworks on the pages that follow that do not have a handy, simple formula. But they do provide important insights into how marketing managers and executives should nurture and care for the brand assets under their responsibility.

MAGIC NUM8ER 11

Revenue

THE DEFINITION

Unless a startlingly new definition has been developed, revenue is still fundamentally known as the total income from sales of products and services.

THE FORMULA AND ITS COMPONENTS

$R = P \times Q$

Where

R = revenue
P = price
Q = quantity

Price refers to the actual price of all products and services sold, not an average price. This is because you are calculating actual sales, not forecasting possible sales. Quantity is simply the number of units that you sold.

WHERE'S THE DATA?

Revenue figures are found in the income statement. They can be calculated by aggregating sales data from each product's sales results, or by adding each sales rep's total sales (both within a given period of time, usually one year).

CALCULATING IT

If you are selling services, then it may be the hours you worked multiplied by the amount you bill for each hour. Or it may be an agreed fixed fee for a contracted amount of time. An advertising agency, for example, bids for clients based on advertising budgets and the communication objective the client is trying to accomplish. For example, my firm, Brand New View, markets two types of services: customized executive-education programs; and creative-design services. In executive education for one-time clients, we charge either fixed fees per day for a pre-agreed number of days, and/or we charge for an entire program. Our creative-design group, when working with one-time clients, charges based on the total hours/weeks estimated to be needed to accomplish the task, and/or the type of project (multi-media, print ads, web design…). When we are working with clients who seek a longer-term relationship, then we negotiate a contract that outlines the basic understanding of what is to be accomplished and when, plus a host of other variables (definitions of work, measurement, expected outcome, deliverables, hours we are dedicating for that client's discretion).

WHAT IT MEANS AND POTENTIAL CHALLENGES

It is pretty hard to misunderstand what revenue means, but let me suggest that it is not a measure that combines actual business plus "business we came close to getting". I mention this in the wake of the accounting scandals in recent years, when it appeared that even sensible people appeared senseless and re-defined common business practices and terms. From a marketing standpoint, revenue is the first indicator, and often a lead driver, of performance measurement. When launching a new product, forecasting revenues and, upon post-launch review, measuring them, provides a guideline for assessing success. It is, of course, merely a starting point and marketers must resist the temptation to focus only on top-line growth because your financial counterparts are going to be concerned with bottom-line results and the costs that affect them. Therefore, marketers must be concerned with costs as well. The reason I even include revenue as a Magic Number for Consumer Marketing is because it comprises two ingredients vital to marketing: price and quantity; in other words, how much and how many. When marketers start considering the factors that influence price and quantity, then they begin to understand more about the business.

MAGIC NUM8ER

12

Gross Profit

THE DEFINITION

In his book *Magic Numbers: The 33 Key Ratios That Every Investor Should Know*, Peter Temple says that gross profit "…is always the top-most profit figure quoted in the income statement".[1]

THE FORMULA AND ITS COMPONENTS

$$P_g = R - C$$

Where

P_g = gross profits
R = revenues
C = costs

Revenues, as defined here, are the broadest definition of revenues one can imagine: total sales, pure and simple. This includes all sales of all products and services in your company, without exception. The costs at this very high level are inclusive of basic materials and components. It does not include operating costs such as salaries, sales and marketing expenditures and depreciation expenses.

WHERE'S THE DATA?

Gross profit is found in the income statement and follows the Total Sales minus Cost of Sales figures.

CALCULATING IT

How hard can it be? Just take a look at these figures from EBay for the last three years:

PERIOD ENDING	31-Dec-03	31-Dec-02	31-Dec-01
Total Revenue	2,165,096	1,214,100	748,821
Cost of Revenue	416,058	213,876	134,816
Gross Profit	1,749,038	1,000,224	614,005

As you can see, EBay is doing quite well. Don't you wish you had bought its stock in 2001?

Here are the figures for Google, which went public in August 2004:

PERIOD ENDING	31-Dec-03	31-Dec-02
Total Revenue	1,465,934	439,508
Cost of Revenue	625,854	131,510
Gross Profit	840,080	307,998

If you had been fortunate enough to buy shares in Google when it went public, your money would have doubled by now (late 2004 at the time of writing). But this section isn't about investing, it is about gross profit, so let me return to earth and the gist of this section.

WHAT IT MEANS AND POTENTIAL CHALLENGES

Gross profit by itself is merely a general indicator, meaning it doesn't provide deep insight into the overall performance of the company, except to suggest that it is headed in the right direction. From the two examples used above, however, you can already begin to see some exciting trends for both companies. As an investor, that would be a good start. As a marketer, it hopefully indicates that you have momentum in the market and that, as a "caretaker" of the company's marketing success, you ought to ensure your marketing efforts continue to build share, brand and long-term customer loyalty as profitably as possible. Also, as a marketer, you want to know and understand these numbers because it indicates that you are paying attention to something more than just advertising or price promotions.

[1] Temple, Peter, *Magic Numbers: The 33 Key Ratios That Every Investor Should Know*, p.54, John Wiley and Sons ©2002.

Net Profit

THE DEFINITION

This is your final profit after taxes and other income statement take-outs.

THE FORMULA AND ITS COMPONENTS

$$P_n = (V \times M_c) - E_m - E_o - I_t$$

Where

P_n = net profit
V = customer volume
M_c = margin per customer
E_m = marketing expenses
E_o = operating expenses
I_t = interest and taxes

Margin per customer is calculated by the simple formula:

$$M_c = R_c - C_v$$

Where

M_c = margin per customer
R_c = revenue per customer
C_v = variable cost per customer

Customer volume is calculated as follows

$$V_c = MD \times MS$$

Where

V_c = customer volume
M_d = market demand
M_s = market share

WHERE'S THE DATA?

This data will be found in your income statement, but typically at the aggregate level. You would probably need to check with the accounting department to review your accounts receivable to determine the number of customers you have and to calculate the margin per customer from there. Marketing and operating expenses will be captured at the departmental level but, if you work in a larger company, corporate headquarters often "charges" certain costs items to each department, even though they are provided by the main office without input from the departments individually. Interest and taxes are handled by the finance group as well.

CALCULATING IT

Emphatic Enterprises (with its new slogan, "We mean business") sells motivational books and tapes targeted to ambitious young executives. It has the following statistics:

V = 400,000
M_c = \$50
E_m = \$1,500,000
E_o = \$500,000
I_t = \$6,500,000
$N_P = (C_V \times M_c) - E_m - E_o - I_t$
$NP = (400,000 \times \$50) - \$2,500,000 - \$1,500,000 - \$6,500,000$
    = \$9,500,000

Of course, these numbers are not actual, nor is Emphatic Enterprises a real company (as far as I know). But the calculation demonstrates how to determine net profit.

WHAT IT MEANS AND POTENTIAL CHALLENGES

Net profit helps you understand how *truly* profitable your company is *after* accounting for additional, below-the-line expenses that result from your efforts to develop the business. A key challenge is determining your customer-volume and customer-margin figures reasonably accurately. This would require a deep understanding of your actual customer base, their purchasing specifics (to help determine average margin) and a good description of the operating expenses associated with this effort.

Profit Impact

THE DEFINITION

In a marketing context, this refers to the effect on profits of your product and marketing expenditure decisions. It affects the gross profits number we discussed in Magic Number 12.

THE FORMULA AND ITS COMPONENTS

Profit impact $= (C_{pu} \times U_s) - C_{fc}$

Where

C_{pu} = contribution per unit
U_s = units sold
C_{fc} = total fixed costs

WHERE'S THE DATA?

As outlined in the customer acquisition/breakeven/LTVC sections (see Magic Numbers 30–32), the C_{pu} information will be found in your retail and wholesale pricing and margin data. This can usually be found in both the finance and marketing departments, if the marketing people are on the ball. The same is true with the information pertaining to units sold. If you are struggling to get timely data, then you can also go to your sales department and get their most recent figures since those may not have been forwarded to the finance and accounting groups yet. The fixed costs would also be in the financial figures, but could be derived from department-by-department research on your own.

CALCULATING IT

Profit impact $= (C_{pu} \times U_s) - C_{fc}$

Using the figures from Ming's Squeezable wallets again (see Magic Number 10), we get the following results:

Profit impact $= (\$3.40 \times 7,000,000) - \$2,050,000$
$$= \$21,750,000$$

The fixed-cost figure assumes she hires consultants and adds to her $1,800,000 fixed-costs amount.

WHAT IT MEANS AND POTENTIAL CHALLENGES

The profit-impact figure gives you a sense of the effect your marketing expenditures have on the profitability of your company or, in the case of Ming, her product line. The challenges are, of course, that it still does not paint an entirely accurate picture of marketing's impact, other than from a predominantly cost standpoint. As frustrating as this is, marketing expenditures in the period of time measured are not always felt by consumers in the market at the same time. There is usually longer-term, residual benefit from marketing activities undertaken today, unless the expenditures are devoted purely to short-term promotional incentives designed to pump up revenues and demand now. If that is the case, it is unlikely (although possible) that these promotional efforts will have a lasting impact and will carry over from one period to the next. Although unlikely, there is a slight possibility that this could happen because almost every activity a company pursues creates some sort of impression in the market, even if it is designed to have a finite life. For example, in Singapore there is a department store called Robinsons, which holds regular sales for short periods of time. Customers are likely being trained to buy mostly during the sale periods, which means that between sales, despite the lack of marketing communication, they are expecting promotions about the next sale because they have been trained to expect them. This behavior, though, is by no means exclusive to Robinsons — indeed, it is common to the promotional efforts of most retailers.

Earnings-Based Value

THE DEFINITION

My financial colleagues who live and breathe this stuff think that this is one of those measures that make the world go around. Frankly, I find that hard to believe, but understanding brand-value based on this can be a helpful exercise in assessing whether a project or even an acquisition is attractive and will add value to your firm.

So what is earnings-based value? To answer this, you have to go through a semi-tortuous sequence only Satan or a CFO could love. It begins with EPS (earnings per share), leads to the P/E (price/earnings) ratio, is applied to the PEG (the price/earnings growth) and YPEG (the year-ahead price/earnings growth) ratios and, PRESTO!!, you have a sense of the value based on earnings. But before you get through this chain of hellish events, it is helpful to understand a key definition: earnings. Earnings means the same thing as net profit or net income and it equates to the money that remains once a business has covered all costs and paid its bills. It is reasonably common practice to assess earnings based on EPS.

While marketers and finance people rarely share the same view of the world, there being no guarantees or certainties even with "precise" measures such as this, future growth opportunities are what make either a new product or an acquisition attractive to companies and shareholders and these formulas help determine future value.

THE FORMULAS AND THEIR COMPONENTS

EPS

To determine EPS, divide the actual dollars earned (or whatever currency you use) by the number of shares outstanding.

P/E Ratio

The P/E ratio takes the most recent stock price and divides it by the most recent four quarters of cumulative earnings.

This gives the price per share (PPS), which is then divided by earnings per share (EPS)

PEG Ratio

The PEG ratio compares earnings growth to the P/E ratio. It does so by taking the historical annualized rate of growth and compares it with the current stock price. PEG is most typically used for younger, rapidly growing companies. It was a common ratio during the booming dot.com era, for example. Theoretically, as long as your P/E ratio does not exceed your growth rate, then your company is reasonably valued. A PEG of .5 to 1.0 is considered good or fair value, whereas a PEG of greater than 1.0 indicates that the company is probably overvalued.

The PEG is equal to the current P/E ratio divided by the historical earnings growth rate:

$$PEG = \frac{P/E}{\text{EPS Historical Growth}}$$

YPEG Ratio

The YPEG ratio uses the same basic assumptions as the PEG ratio, but bases it on projected future growth rates and not the PEG ratio's historical rates. YPEG is more commonly used for larger, more mature companies. The same logic applies as with the PEG ratio: .5 to 1.0 is good and greater than 1.0 is a potential problem.

The YPEG ratio equals the current P/E ratio divided by the future earnings growth rate:

$$YPEG = \frac{P/E}{\text{EPS Future Growth}}$$

WHERE'S THE DATA?

As with earlier definitions, publicly traded companies have this information in their annual reports, typically in their financial statements in the sections called "Notes to Financial Statements" or "Notes to Consolidated Financial Statements".

CALCULATING IT

EPS

Let's assume your company is called "Boring Widgets" (BW) and it has five million shares outstanding and has earned $2.5 million in the previous 12 months. Then BW's trailing EPS is 50 cents

$$\frac{\$2,500,000}{5,000,000 \text{ shares}} = .5$$

Don't get too excited about having completed the obvious math. By itself, EPS is relatively unhelpful and only becomes more important as you include it into the rest of the earnings valuation analysis.

P/E Ratio

Now, let's assume that BW has a stock price of $50 per share. Using our new-found fancy formulas and math skills, we find

$$\frac{\$50}{0.5} = 100$$

100 is the P/E. Now it is time to get excited! Why? Because you have a P/E that is similar to the dot.coms in their heyday, so you are well on your way to paper wealth that will begin burning a hole in your virtual pocket.

PEG Ratio

Using BW once again as our example and assuming, for the sake of completing the analysis, that the historical growth rate is 25% this gives us the following:

$$PEG = \frac{P/E}{EPS \text{ Historical Growth}}$$
$$= \frac{100}{25}$$
$$= 4.0$$

The PEG is 4.0. This indicates that Boring Widgets is overvalued and is worth four times what it should be.

YPEG Ratio

Completing our BW illustration, but assuming that it is now a more mature firm and that growth is expected to be closer to 10% in the coming years, produces the following result:

$$YPEG = \frac{P/E}{EPS \text{ Future Growth}}$$
$$= \frac{100}{10}$$
$$= 10.0$$

The YPEG is 10.0. (Trust me, you have a problem).

What it Means and Potential Challenges

Earnings-based values are complex and make certain assumptions that are fine theoretically, but are not always relevant or even practical in the real world. It is prudent to recognize that earnings-based values reflect only a subset of the potential value a firm, brand or product represents. By themselves, they are interesting and helpful, but hardly conclusive or prescriptive. Yet the danger is that many business decisions are made based on this information. Businesses are more than an earnings stream. In fact, earnings, in their simplest form, are merely a measure of success during a particular period of time. Economics assumes a rational consumer in many of its theories, yet in reality many consumer decisions are made based on a combination of intuition, logic and plain old guesswork, effectively blowing traditional economics right out of the water. Similarly, earnings-based valuations assume that the ideal world is one in which the P/E ratio and the EPS growth rate are equal, or should be very close to equal. Unfortunately for those of you who are logical thinkers, we live in a world that is messy and unpredictable, making you feel uncomfortable and ill at ease. While a 1.0 sounds appealing, BW has a YPEG of 10.0 and to many investors that may seem perfectly reasonable, as does a P/E of 100. Go figure. Then again, why do some people spend $10,000 on a Rolex, when a perfectly good Timex can be purchased for $10, even though they operate on the same mechanics (essentially)? Ah, for us marketers, the world is a wondrous place filled with opportunity and irreconcilable contradictions waiting to be exploited. What fun would it be if everything were perfectly predictable and understood?

16

Return on Sales

THE DEFINITION

Return on sales (ROS) is a measure of efficiency based on a company's ability to generate profits from sales.

It is based on net profit after tax and total sales. ROS helps companies determine the effectiveness of their sales to drive profitability. It is also a measure of management's effectiveness.

THE FORMULA AND ITS COMPONENTS

$$ROS = \frac{P_{nat}}{S}$$

Where

ROS = return on sales
P_{nat} = net profit after tax
S = sales

WHERE'S THE DATA?

The income statement is the best place to find this information.

CALCULATING IT

As we saw in Magic Number 13, Emphatic Enterprises is quite successful. Its motivational products generated $300,000,000 in sales,

which means there is a market of people seeking exhortations that they
"CAN do it!". Emphatic certainly did it. At least, in terms of sales, it did.

$$\text{ROS} = \frac{\$9,500,000}{\$300,000,000} = 3.1\%$$

These figures may indicate that Emphatic needs to improve its margins.
On the other hand, Emphatic's market characteristics may also suggest
that 3.1% is a reasonable ROS.

WHAT IT MEANS AND POTENTIAL CHALLENGES

ROS is a practical indicator of the profitability of your marketing efforts.
However, as Emphatic grows, it may want to focus more on increasing
margin to take advantage of the investment and effort made to produce
its current line of products.

Return on Assets

THE DEFINITION

Return on assets (ROA) is a measure of efficiency based on a company's ability to generate profits from its existing assets.

THE FORMULA AND ITS COMPONENTS

$$ROA = \frac{P_{nat}}{A}$$

Where

ROA = return on assets
P_{nat} = net profit after tax
A = assets

WHERE'S THE DATA?

The income statement will have information on the net profit after tax. The balance sheet will have information on assets.

CALCULATING IT

Those analytical folks at Emphatic Enterprises are not satisfied assessing their return on sales. They also want to understand the management's effectiveness in getting as much productivity and profitability out of their assets as possible). The company's assets have skyrocketed in value and it is sitting on a rich treasure trove of products, manufacturing, education programs and similar things. Total assets now total $425,347,333 (how's that for precision?).

$$ROA = \frac{\$9,500,000}{\$425,347,333} = 2.2\%$$

WHAT IT MEANS AND POTENTIAL CHALLENGES

As you consider this 2.2% figure, you may be scratching your head and wondering, "Is that a good figure?" Good question. Generally speaking, the higher the number, the better. Some industries may see any number greater than 1% as a good ROA number (really slow, dull businesses, for example). On the other hand, a technology company may see 8% or more as a reasonable indicator of effectiveness for that sector. Just be aware that ROA by itself is a helpful indicator, but it is better to appraise it in the context of your industry and your main competitor set. You may feel perfectly good about 8%, but if the competitors are at 11 or 12%, then you may have to take a closer look at your business.

Return on Equity

THE DEFINITION

Return on equity (ROE) is a measure of efficiency based on a company's ability to generate profits from its stockholders' equity.

THE FORMULA AND ITS COMPONENTS

$$ROE = \frac{P_{nat}}{E}$$

Where

ROE = return on equity
P_{nat} = net profit after tax
E   = equity

WHERE'S THE DATA?

The balance sheet liabilities will tell you the equity values.

CALCULATING IT

This is getting quite interesting. Emphatic Enterprises wants even more information to measure management's effectiveness. The board is under pressure from investors and financial analysts because, as it turns out, its 2.2% ROA is well below industry average. The board members are all staring at pictures of Emphatic's CEO and developing an unfavorable opinion of her. But to avoid a hasty or imprudent decision, they run another calculation, this time based on owner's equity. As it turns out, Emphatic Enterprise has $92 million in owner's equity.

$$ROE = \frac{\$9,500,000}{\$92,000,000} = 10.3\%$$

What it Means and Potential Challenges

As it turns out, an ROE of 10.3% is above average for the industry, so the stockholders are quite happy for now, which means the board of directors is happy as well. However, they remain concerned about the low ROA and ROS ratios and are telling the CEO she must focus on improving effectiveness and profitability in those areas if she wants to keep her job. They give her a year to demonstrate improvement.

ROE has limitations as a measure of effectiveness, however. It looks at the amount of invested capital as assets minus liabilities (this is the traditional definition of owner's equity). In less financial techno-speak, this means it does not fully account for all invested capital accurately. There is debt in the form of both short-term and long-term financial capital. So a more complete analysis would measure the return on invested capital to give investors and the board a clearer picture of the effectiveness of invested capital to generate profits. However, that is a topic that, fortunately, falls outside the remit of this book.

Note on Brand Value and Brand Equity

An active debate rages about the two Magic Numbers for Consumer Marketing that follow. This results from differing interpretations of how to measure the impact of brand on a company's performance and value. The debate is whether these are really two separate concepts, or one. There are marketing practitioners and academics who suggest these two terms are really just the same concept, with only semantic differences. Those on this side of the debate see these two concepts strictly as a financial measure. On the other side of the debate are those who believe that these two concepts are related, but separate. This latter group tends to define brand value as a combination of financial measures and intangible effects and sees brand equity as a financial tool that helps determine overall brand value. Neither of these is 100%

precise nor universally agreed upon. Furthermore, there are merits to viewing both concepts as distinct, so I have chosen to present both. Finally, my own experience and research suggests that brand is a far more complex topic than can be adequately captured by a mere formula, so you now have a sense of my bias in this debate.

Brand-Value Frameworks

Congratulations. You have already gotten this far in the book and are still interested. That's good because it means you realize that the Magic Numbers for Consumer Marketing are not hard and fast, singular or crisp definitions. Instead, by now you have discovered that marketing's Magic Numbers are really a series of measurement categories, based partly on traditional finance formulas and ratios, and partly on your interpretation of a business situation and your perception of the market. It is important to come to this realization because now we enter the turbulent, and sometimes confusing, waters known as brand-value.

The topic of brand-value is complex for one simple reason: you are measuring an intangible. It is a bit like measuring air. You know it is important, but pinning down a precise dollar value is challenging. Except that you know that without it you cannot survive. In a similar, but admittedly less dire, fashion, brand-value is important to the firm. Some might argue that they do not need a valuable brand for their business to make money, and they are probably right. But there is a sizable chasm between firms that merely survive and those that thrive. As brand experts will tell you, companies with a well-regarded brand return a premium on their market value over their lesser-known competitors. Many firms make money. Few are truly successful from a brand-value standpoint.[1]

To give you a deeper perspective on brand-value, I will describe five approaches. As you will see, each offers insight about how to assess brand-value and each is highly subjective. There is some overlap between the approaches, yet each offers something unique that provokes curiosity. In some cases, brand-value and brand equity are treated synonymously, and others define them as distinctly different. I will explain after we examine each one.

THE BROAD DEFINITION

This is commonly understood to be the premium attached to added contribution from intangible assets including goodwill, share price and market performance. None of these are physical assets. Instead, they represent the perceived value beyond the book value of the tangible assets.

In this context, brand-value is determined based on a variation of the accountant's balance sheet. Brand-value is simply the difference between your firm's brand assets and its brand liabilities. On the left side of this classic model are brand assets and on the right side are brand-value and brand liabilities, with each side balancing the other. Conceptually, this is useful imagery in that it conveys brand-value in a model familiar to most business people. But this description leaves a great deal of room for interpretation. Specifically, what *is* a brand asset, what goes *into* brand-value and what *is* a brand liability. Furthermore, some would suggest that this definition is known as "brand equity", since it follows the accounting balance-sheet methodology. However, we will discuss brand equity separately as the next Magic Number. To clarify brand-value, let's look at an example.

Philip Morris and Kraft

In the late 1980s, Philip Morris purchased Kraft for $12.9 billion and this was considered a reasonable price for a company with as valuable a brand name as Kraft. A closer look at this transaction reveals that the tangible assets were valued at $1.3 billion. Thus, Kraft's brand was truly valuable since it accounted for the other $11.6 billion. Accounting convention sometimes describes this as "goodwill". Whatever word you use, it means the same thing: there is a premium attached to the concept of brand. One of the most interesting questions is what creates this perception of premium value. Certainly, *trust* is a dominant influence on the perception of a company, its products and its brand. Customers are not likely to buy products or services from a source they consider untrustworthy. Yet how does one measure trust? It is a bit like the concept of beauty — you understand it implicitly even if your description and tangible illustration differs from that of the person next to you. One can thus infer that the better known and respected a brand, the higher the premium it can command. This may not always hold true, but it is certainly true much of the time. Starbucks, as of FY2003, had $2.7 billion in assets and over $4 billion in revenue. Its market capitalization, however, was over $20 billion.[2] That is a sizable difference over tangible assets. The point is that brand-value is a strategically vital asset, yet it is also exasperatingly hard to measure precisely. Let's review the frameworks.

THE FRAMEWORKS AND THEIR COMPONENTS

Framework: The Young and Rubicam (Y&R) Brand Asset Valuator

Y&R's Brand Asset Valuator consists of four key elements:

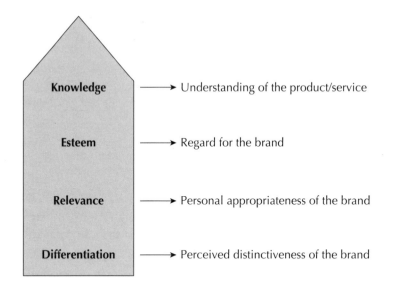

Each element builds upon the previous. Differentiation, the ability to represent uniqueness to the market, is a key element driving the success of any branding effort. Without some level of differentiation, one firm and/or its products is no different from another, thus rendering any value from branding either a waste or unnecessary. Therefore, according to the Y&R model, companies MUST differentiate to begin building brand-value. However, as a business builds its brand, differentiation is only the beginning and could lead a company to a quick end if the offerings are not relevant to the market. The world is littered with differentiated products ("NEW! this", "IMPROVED!! that", "SPECIAL FEATURES!") that lost touch with consumers' needs and therefore lost their interest. But by focusing on relevance, a company is telling consumers that it cares and is making products that are interesting and important to them. Of course, convincing consumers of your distinctiveness through differentiation and of the product's relevance to them creates expectations that the products will work and last. This implies a high level of quality (one could credibly argue that "quality" is the minimum cost of entry in any market these days, even for undifferentiated products). Quality is termed "esteem" by Y&R as it deals with the essence of the product promise itself. For a moment, imagine yourself as a product. The quality of your efforts reflects directly on you and your esteem, both in terms of self and professional impressions as well. Finally, assuming consumers are believers in your company and/or its products, you develop a wider base of knowledge about your offerings that spreads from one happy consumer to the next as they learn of the great products and services you offer. Individually, each of these elements is important to any company. Collectively, these elements comprise Y&R's definition of brand-value. They are useful descriptors of a brand and can serve as a framework for a company's brand-building efforts.

Framework: David Aaker's Brand Model[3]

David Aaker has conducted relevant research into branding over several decades, most recently with his firm, Prophet. His model of brand describes how to build a brand, develop and implement a long-term brand strategy, and track performance.

The core of his model views a company's brand in four areas:

Brand as Product

A company's offerings are the tangible manifestation of the brand. They are often the main connection point to consumers. Every component or ingredient of your offering must be consistent with the overall brand of the company.

Brand as Organization

A company's structure and competencies directly affect the perception of the brand in the market. The organization must be a mirror of the image the market sees when it "meets" your brand. This includes how employees handle interactions with customers and suppliers.

Brand as Symbol

This refers to a brand's tried and true imagery: its logo, colors, slogan. But brand as symbol also references a brand's link to celebrities or other status associations. Each of these represents the brand symbolically.

Brand as Person

When asked to describe somebody, we often begin with their personality or their behavior or the various qualities that they represent. In a company context, the concept of person or personality is equally descriptive. Companies are "innovative" (3M), or "cautious" (financial services) or "empathetic" (services companies such as Banyan Tree Hotels).

Aaker's model has numerous other dimensions that also shape a brand, but it is useful to contemplate your own company's brand in regard to these four areas. In fact, one could argue that Y&R's Brand Asset Valuator and Aaker's model can be blended to offer more depth either to the qualitative dimensions of the Y&R model or the tangible dimensions of Aaker's model. Either way, the astute business person will recognize that brand is not merely a name or an invisible, hard-to-grasp, accounting category and that it is a complex set of assets that, ideally, integrate with each other to create a holistic representation of the company to the market. There are more ways to look at brand, however.

Framework: Brand Finance's Brand Valuation[4]

Brand Finance is a respected U.K.-based brand valuation consultancy that uses the following framework for assessing brand-value.

- Market analysis: to understand brands, competitors and overall market conditions
- Brand financial analysis: to determine branded business earnings

- Driver analysis: to determine what proportion of business earnings are attributable to the brand (Brand Finance incorporates a concept called Brand-Value Added, or BVA™, which is derived from economic value added, EVA, and a combination of market data, company financial data and demand drivers)

- Brand risk review: assesses the risk factor (beta) associated with the earnings (using a tool called βrandβeta™, which incorporates 10 objective indicators of brand performance).

The Brand Finance methodology then distills the results from these four areas into a valuation for the brand. It assesses the added value attributed to the brand after tax, discounting it at a rate consistent with the brand's risk profile to determine a brand-value.

Framework: Interbrand's Brand Valuation Methodology[5]

Interbrand is one of the leading firms in brand valuation. For years, its model has been very influential in helping companies determine how to value their respective brands using a methodology that is based on the income approach, which defines brand-value as the discounted future cash flow derived from the future earnings stream. Essentially, determining brand-value requires companies to understand the profits they derive from their branded products as compared to the profits of companies with a lesser-known or unknown brand. Additionally, calculating the value of a brand name based on royalties earned by products carrying that brand name can be a component of the income approach. Finally, companies must know the costs (fixed, variable, taxes) that are involved in directly supporting the brand.

Interbrand uses a variation of the income approach partly because it wanted a model that included well-known financial and accounting concepts, which provide a measure of tangible reassurance with an otherwise intangible asset. But there is more to Interbrand's approach. The company sought to encompass less-understood, but often equally important, dimensions of a brand — the investment in marketing and the legal protections required to maintain brand integrity and intellectual property against competitors. The reason for this is that each of these dimensions influences the perception and, ultimately, the value of a brand. Brand is not, as already cautioned earlier, a name or logo.

Interbrand's methodology attempts to reflect the complex characteristics that create and sustain a brand.

Interbrand evaluates brands across seven factors, and its methodology works through five steps. The seven factors (and their weights) Interbrand reviews are:

1. Leadership (25%)

As the term implies, leadership reflects the brand's ability to set and/or guide the direction of a product category, market or industry. Brands in leadership positions establish price, product quality, perception and even expectations about future offerings. Consequently, brands in leadership positions are considered premier and can command premium product pricing and company value over lesser-known rivals.

2. Stability (15%)

Perhaps this could also be termed "durability" and/or "resilience". In their influential 1994 book *Built to Last*, James C. Collins and Jerry I. Porras wrote about how, over years, even generations, a select group of companies had built enduring legacies of success. While some of the firms they profiled have either been eclipsed by other firms or their performance has wavered a bit, the fundamental concepts they describe set a reliable foundation for long-term success. Great brands must have long-term success and stability is a key factor as a result.

3. Market (10%)

A brand's market is essentially the environmental and business context in which it operates. Many variables influence this, including type of industry (auto, education, consumer products, software). Each industry is directly driven by its own unique dynamics. The pace of product innovation in hotels is far slower than that of computers. The loyalty of customers is often more intense in sophisticated technologies than it is for hairspray. Of course, investment in time, resources and money influences this type of loyalty, and not all indicators of loyalty mean that customers are necessarily happy. Nevertheless, market is a key factor in determining brand-value.

4. Geographic spread (25%)

Companies with established global operations often find it easier to introduce similar products in different regions and cultures as a result of market perception, consumer expectations and general recognition of the brand. With this kind of operating scale, large MNCs (multinational companies) are usually more valuable than their region-specific counterparts, partly because the MNCs have developed capabilities that allow their products to be more easily accepted across diverse cultures.

5. Trend (10%)

The concept of trend often carries with it connotations of the fickle, the fleeting, the ephemeral and, unfortunately at times, the insubstantial. Yet trends are either set or supported by consumers. Consumer embracement of new trends reflects changes in society and companies must pay attention if they wish to remain relevant. A strong brand must be relevant to consumers or it, too, will only be a fad.

6. Support (10%)

From marketing communications to R&D, brands need a steady stream of care, maintenance and investment. Much like people who need food and water to survive through good times and bad, brands must also receive nourishment from support, in good times and bad, to survive.

7. Protection (5%)

Companies spend sizable amounts of money developing products, building identities, communicating to consumers and developing their organizations to support the brand. It is foolhardy not to protect your brand name, product or other intellectual property from competitors who hope to take what you have built. Furthermore, investors expect companies to protect their brands since this directly affects brand-value and investor value.

Interbrand regularly measures the market on behalf of companies and their brands through surveys and similar research in an effort to understand each of these factors as thoroughly and thoughtfully as possible. It scores the results and translates them into an earnings multiple. Much like assessing a company's risk profile in financial terms, Interbrand calculates a brand's return compared to low- and high-risk investments.

A five-step process is used throughout the review of the seven factors.

1. Market Segmentation

Define clear, non-overlapping segments. The brand is then valued in each segment and the cumulative value of all segments equals the total brand-value.

2. Financial Analysis

Revenues and profits for each segment's brand intangibles are identified and forecast.

3. Demand Analysis

Determine the drivers of demand for each of the company's brands and segments, then assess how much each driver is directly influenced by the brand.

4. Competitive Benchmarking

An extensive review of the competitive position of the company's brands, including leadership, strengths and weaknesses, growth trends, legal protectability, geographic spread and related items is undertaken. This is done to determine the brand discount rate and the risk profile of its future expected earnings.

5. Brand-Value Calculation

Interbrand defines this as the net present value of the forecast brand earnings, discounted by the brand discount rate. The net present value takes into consideration both the forecast period and beyond, to model the brand's ability to continue generating quality future earnings.

This overview only covers the highlights of Interbrand's model, but you can certainly see its comprehensive design and its use of established finance methodologies, adapted for specific brand measurement. This can help CFOs and CEOs feel a bit more relaxed since the model is grounded in approaches with which they are familiar. Of course, there is a fair amount of rigorous, in-depth analysis needed to address each of the seven factors and five steps, so it is not a "back of the envelope" calculation. It serves to illustrate the complexity of valuing brands and the strategic importance a brand has on the overall value, perception and performance of a company.

Interbrand's methodology has the advantage of being widely accepted and used, in large part due to its comprehensive design. It captures several critical areas of the firm. David Aaker praises the Interbrand approach for its effort to put a financial value on the brand, but cautions, "The subjectivity of both the criteria and the assessment of the brands, however, makes the dimensions difficult to defend and affects the reliability of the resulting measures."[6] In other words, despite its analytical rigor, the Interbrand methodology is not perfect. Then again, few business formulas and frameworks are perfect.

Framework: WPP BrandDynamics Pyramid

This model is similar to the Y&R Brand Asset Valuator. In the WPP BrandDynamics Pyramid, the relationship between the brand and its consumers is measured against the share of the consumer's wallet that the brand has. Share of wallet is a concept that will be more thoroughly defined later in this book.

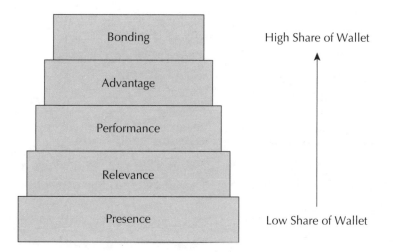

As you move up the pyramid, the consumer's relationship with the brand deepens.

- Presence merely describes a general awareness of, but little commitment to, the brand.

- Relevance indicates that the consumer finds the brand offers something of interest and may lead to an increased commitment.

- Performance indicates increased usage and growing confidence that the consumer finds the brand useful.

- Advantage implies that the consumer identifies more closely with the brand and that the brand offers some advantage that the consumer finds attractive.

- Finally, bonding describes the deepest relationship between the brand and the consumer, where the consumer is a committed user of the brand and will select that brand first when purchasing. It also implies that the consumer feels a strong affinity for the imagery the brand represents.

WPP's model suggests that there is a definable size at each step of the pyramid and that is indeed the case. Each step is sized according to the number of consumers in that stage. It stands to reason that as a brand's relationship with its consumers intensifies, there are fewer consumers who are at the top of the pyramid simply because not everyone who is aware at the bottom is likely to move up the pyramid to become highly bonded. Other brands and competitors will vie for their attention, creating a natural attrition of sorts. Ideally, a brand would like to see the number of consumers at the Bonding level as were originally at the Presence level, as this may well indicate that its marketing efforts to develop its customer base are working. (That is not the only conclusion one would reach, but it is certainly worthy of investigation.)

Framework: Brand New View Brand Architecture

In the past few years, much of my work has been devoted to helping companies develop their brand strategy, through consulting, design and executive-education programs. Included with this has been teaching at the University of Washington's Business School in its EMBA, TMMBA (technology management MBA) and Executive Education programs, at UC Davis's Executive Education program and currently at Singapore Management University. Throughout this time, I have researched dozens of companies overall, interviewed CEOs and senior executives and have analyzed marketing and branding efforts at companies in North America and Asia. Prior to this, I spent nearly 20 years of my career as a manager, executive and entrepreneur, seeing how companies work from the inside and noting strengths and weaknesses throughout. While my role was most often outwardly focused to the market through developing product and marketing plans and programs, it was apparent that each company needed to turn its marketing inward toward its own employees if it was to match the perceptions it was building in the marketplace. While this is hardly revolutionary news, it is surprising how few firms actually do this. The notion of developing passionate, devoted employees and a culture that reflects the true nature of the brand is mostly given lip service. Of these experiences, Nike stood out as a company that believed in building its brand internally as well as externally and, to this day, I would argue that this is a key reason why it is the world leader and has been for nearly two decades. Nike certainly pays attention to financial performance, but it recognizes the critical role that people play in creating financial success. This combination of branding both inside and out is one of the reasons I refer to the company frequently in this book.

From these experiences and research, it became clear that there are four central themes that both define and dictate a company's brand direction. Each of these has its own sub-framework that helps companies build a complete plan for its brand direction, creating a Brand Matrix Architecture that captures essential requirements needed to build successful brands. Further exploration into each of the four themes includes a penetrating brand audit designed to help companies understand where time, energy and resources can be deployed to benefit the development of a strong, sustainable brand. However, for the purposes of this book it is sufficient to capture just the main themes.

The four key elements of the model are:

• Destiny

Destiny is an expansive concept that describes the core characteristics of the brand and/or company and answers thematic questions related to corporate philosophy, "*Why* is the organization here?" and "What is the organization's personality? '*Who*' is this organization?" Destiny is analogous to the reason for the organization to exist, as discussed by Collins and Porras in *Built to Last*. However, destiny encompasses not just the organization's *raison d'être*, but also its soul. Destiny is an important area for an organization to understand for a few simple reasons: if a company does not know why it is here, then it is unlikely to know where it can go, what it can do and which opportunities it should exploit. Articulating and understanding destiny is as necessary for organizations as it is for people…without a purpose, there is no direction. Without a clear self-definition, there is little chance of developing recognized expertise. Companies that do not understand their destiny risk becoming faceless to the market and their message will lack clarity (since there will be little understanding of what is necessary to communicate).

• Culture

When one considers culture at the country level, it is fairly easy to describe the characteristics that help define it. Mention France and most people immediately conjure images and ideas closely linked with its culture (art, politics, cuisine, language). The same is true for a company, albeit on a less grand scale. Culture answers *who* is involved; consequently, it is concerned with people issues since people create and perpetuate the culture. Culture also addresses how people are supposed to behave inside the company. Nike, Apple, Starbucks, Sony, Danone, L'Oreal, Foster's, BMW and Cirque du Soleil are all examples of companies whose cultures are understood, even if consumers do not regularly buy the products. Having a clearly defined culture is potentially an enormously beneficial asset since talented people will seek a company whose culture matches their interests. Also, culture defines how people within learn, both formally and informally. Thus, culture is increasingly important for employees as they look beyond merely making money and look toward lifestyle, quality of work, and inspiration from those with whom they work.

- Strategy

Simply put, strategy is concerned with where the company is going. Not how it will get there, but simply where it is headed. Strategy is the vehicle for translating destiny into more tangible objectives for the next few years. In effect, it is the longer-term steps a company takes to get closer to its destiny. A word of caution is important here. Strategy does not necessarily have to be lengthy or statistically dense. It can simply be a clear set of directional objectives, including the firm's understanding of its target markets and how it is positioned to address opportunities. While strategy must address existing competitive challenges, it is becoming increasingly important to identify and describe latent needs, such as entirely new markets that competitors are presently ignoring. Finally, performance controls are used to fine-tune a company's path toward its destiny. Reviews of its brand position, in particular, should be undertaken in this area every couple of years.

- Design

This is more complex concept than typical business definitions because it deals with the active and consistent coordination of all aspects of design throughout the company as it evolves its brand. Design involves product decisions (Which products? What should they look like? Which markets? What price?), communication and perception issues

(What should we tell the market and how should we do it?), and tactical controls (Who owns each program and how will it be measured?). Interestingly, design increasingly encompasses issues around physical design (not just product packaging, but the physical office environment and what customers and suppliers see when visiting the firm).

You may have noticed four additional terms in the diagram: "company-facing", "market-facing", "ambition" and "action". Let me describe these briefly:

- "Company-facing" refers to the combination of destiny and culture in creating perceptions, behaviors and social systems that affect those inside the company.

- "Market-facing" reflects the activities resulting from the combination of strategy and design, both of which are manifested in directional choices and programs that directly affect consumers.

- "Ambition" describes the collective passion and desire to achieve arising from destiny and strategy, which combine to create the brand's sense of urgency and purpose in the marketplace.

- "Action" illustrates the specific activities undertaken by the people (culture) who implement the programs (design).

WHERE'S THE DATA?

Much of the data that drives these models is research driven, and is directed by the needs of the company as it seeks to better understand its products and the competitors in the market. Even the brand financial data is derived from the research, and then classic finance models such as net present value and discounted cash flow are applied to determine the value of a brand in a particular market. None of this data is easily found in normal accounting or marketing plans as it is dependent on several different factors, all of which influence the final measure of brand-value.

WHAT THEY MEAN AND POTENTIAL CHALLENGES

As surprising as it may seem, this is not an exhaustive list of brand-valuation techniques. It is apparent that brand valuation is not a precise science, nor can it be, because of the many intangible qualities that influence a brand. However, despite the complexity and inherent subjectivity, it is critical that companies take brand valuation seriously and not jump to the traditional (and quite insufficient) accounting measure known as goodwill. For companies to keep building brand-value, they must strive to understand the complex interdependencies that affect brands. Ignoring them because they are fuzzy, or hard, or too subjective is lazy and potentially dangerous for the business. Each of these brand valuation models requires a vigilant effort from management to monitor the sources of their competitive success and the reasons for weakness. In effect, they have to pay attention to such things as people, work atmosphere and organizational alignment behind company strategy.

This leads to another influence on brand-value: loyalty. This is discussed in Magic Number 26. But very briefly, a fair amount of research indicates that Loyalty tends to be more stable for market leaders. Market leaders also tend to be better known than competitors. In all probability, market leaders have higher brand-value than competitors. Therefore, brand-value and loyalty are likely to be closely linked. Furthermore, loyalty and brand-value are also connected to brand equity, as you will see next.

---

[1] For more reading on this topic, review the books by any of the following business authors as they delve deeply into this issue: Kevin Keller at Dartmouth, Bernd Schmitt at Columbia, David Aaker at UC Berkeley, Jim Collins of The Laboratory, Jerry Porras at Stanford Graduate School of Business, Phil Kotler at Northwestern, Tom Peters of The Tom Peters Group and Scott Bedbury of BrandStream.

[2] Yahoo! Business, November 2004.

[3] Aaker, David, *Building Strong Brands*, ©*1996 The Free Press* pp.78–85.

[4] Haigh, David, "Understanding the Financial Value of Brands", 1999 p.10. http://brandfinance.com/pdfs/research/eaaa.pdf

[5] Source: Lindemann, Jan, Managing Director Interbrand Valuations Practice, www.poolonline.com, Issue 24, Autumn 2003, p. 2.

[6] Aaker, op. cit., p.314.

MAGIC NUM8ER

20

Brand Equity

THE DEFINITION

As you will notice frequently in this book, there is sometimes more than one definition of a Magic Number. This is due to the intangible, qualitative factors that are part of the overall marketing assessment. Brand equity, too, has several interpretations.

Phil Kotler describes brand equity as:

"…the positive differential effect that knowing the brand name has on customer response to the product or service. Brand equity results in customers showing a preference for one product over another when they are basically identical. The extent that customers are willing to pay more for the particular brand is a measure of brand equity."

Kevin Keller describes brand equity in reference to the consumer like this:

"Customer-based brand equity is formally defined as the differential effect the brand knowledge has on consumer response to the marketing of that brand."

Roland Rust, Valerie Zeithaml and Katherine Lemon define brand equity as:

"(The) customers' subjective and intangible assessment of the brand, above and beyond its objectively perceived value. Three key drivers of brand equity are customer brand awareness, customer brand attitudes, and customer perception of brand ethics."

For David Aaker, brand equity is:

"A set of assets and liabilities linked to a brand, its name and symbol that add to or subtract from the value provided by a product or service to a firm and/or that firm's customers."

Roger J. Best views brand equity as the analog to the owner's equity in the balance sheet, except that brand equity is determined by subtracting brand liabilities from brand assets.

Each definition is similar, but slightly different. In some cases, brand equity is seen as more of a pure intangible and in others it is measured as if one were measuring the items on a balance sheet. Which one is correct? They all are!

THE FORMULAS AND THEIR COMPONENTS

There are two approaches to brand equity that I will describe: the first is a framework and the second is more formula-driven. Each approach has unique differences.

Approach 1

David Aaker's "Brand Equity Ten"[1] is a set of brand equity measures organized into five themes. The first four are customer-specific measures based on perception, and the fifth is a more general market-based set of measures, as follows.

Loyalty measures

1. Price premium: this is the price difference a customer is willing to pay for a brand compared to another company's offering in a similar product category.

2. Satisfaction/Loyalty: as the name implies, this helps measure customer loyalty to a specific brand.

Perceived quality/leadership measures

3. Perceived quality: this is admittedly a fuzzier measure, but an important one as well. Simply, it is the consumer's perception of quality associated with a brand. One person's experience with a

product or brand may differ from another's but, on balance, high perceived quality is an important factor in determining brand equity.

4. Leadership/Popularity: leadership can be both literal (as in the top-selling brand in its category) and perceived (trends can often vault a brand to popularity, creating the impression that it is a leader, even if numerically it is not).

Associations/differentiation measures

5. Perceived Value: this describes the value proposition, or benefits to the consumer, rather than the features. To be a leading brand commanding premium prices, it must offer value beyond the competitor's offering.

6. Brand Personality: we regularly describe people's personalities — she is a "risk-taker", he is "shy" — and the same is true for companies. A brand personality connects to consumers and makes the company seem more real and approachable.

7. Organizational Associations: associations can influence the brand. Is the brand associated with positive or negative things? Is the brand partnered with other good brands?

Awareness measures

8. Brand Awareness: this is concerned with the level of awareness consumers have of the brand. Awareness can be further divided into Recall and Recognition, which are described in more detail in Magic Numbers 22 and 23.

Market-behavior measures

9. Market Share: as described in Magic Number 4

10. Market Price and Distribution Coverage: in this context, price describes the relative market price of the brand compared to competitors. Distribution coverage is, of course, concerned with how easy it is for consumers to find the products (i.e. is the brand accessible in different channels?).

Aaker's approach is a development framework rather than a precise formulation in which one can input data and then determine a specific result. His approach is designed to stimulate strategic thinking about the firm's brand from which specific tactical programs can be designed to implement the strategy. Clearly, you should recognize a key implication: each company has unique issues, both internally and externally, so it is incumbent on you to develop your brand equity criteria to best fit your needs. Undoubtedly, this will make those of you who love formulas and statistics squeamish since it requires stepping out of the world of black and white and into the world of gray. But Aaker's approach is a useful organizational construct to help get the brand equity discussion going. Sure, we'd all love to follow a precise recipe, but some of the best chefs do just the opposite. They take their base understanding and interpret recipes creatively to develop dishes that aren't formulaic repeats, but unique signature dishes.

However, for those of you who prefer following a recipe (or painting by numbers, depending on your preferred analogy), then read the next approach. Please leave your right-brain with the doorman.

Approach 2

Deborah MacInnis, Professor of Marketing at USC's Marshall School of Business, and C. Whan Park, the Joseph A. DeBell Professor of Marketing at USC's Marshall School of Business, describe brand equity "as the financial value of brand reflecting its efficiency in attracting and retaining customers".[2] They suggest evaluating brand equity as one would evaluate other financial variables. Their point is that equity has a very specific meaning based on financial valuation techniques and, therefore, should not be subjected to the uncertainties associated with intangibles like consumer perception since those are harder to quantify. In a strict sense, they have a point. It is very hard to place a value on one's perceptions since they are highly subjective.

MacInnis and Park suggest brand equity be examined from both the revenue and costs sides of the business. First, with regard to revenues, since one purpose of any business is to attract and retain customers, then generating revenues is dependent on price. Assuming a company's brand has value (compared to the competitors), then it stands to reason that the brand can command not only a higher market share at equivalent prices, but disproportionate revenue increases at lower prices. Therefore, any brand equity measure should include:

$$R = P \times Q_{ne}$$

Where

R = revenues
P = price
Q_{ne} = quantity demand from new and existing customers

Second, the investments made to develop the customer base affect brand equity. Strong brands should be able to develop their customer base more effectively (and, arguably, more efficiently) than lesser-known rivals. Therefore, their brand should provide leverage that makes customer acquisition less costly compared to competitors since the known-brand does not have to spend as much to acquire and retain customers. Over time, known-brands ought to be able to develop their customer base at a lower per-unit cost than before, since the brand is better known than it was at the beginning, making the brand even more valuable to the company.

Thus, as revenues increase and costs decrease due to the leverage provided by a strong brand, then the brand equity should increase as well.

MacInnis and Park offer the following chart to describe brand equity, comparing the industrial accounting method with the marketing accounting method described above. The similarity is obvious, and for those who seek a basic approach to brand equity based on financial and accounting techniques, then this is a useful definition.

Industrial Accounting System	Marketing Accounting System
Total Revenues	Total Revenues
Cost of Goods Sold	*Total Marketing Costs*
Operating Profit	Magnitude of Brand Value
Marketing Expenses	Cost of Goods Sold
Contribution Margin	Contribution Margin

MacInnis and Park caution, however, that this initial brand equity effort is incomplete because it does not account for differences in different-sized firms with differing marketing costs. While brand value is important, it is equally important to determine the return on marketing costs to understand the efficiency of its marketing investments. They illustrate this with the following examples:

CASE 1	Company A	Company B
Total Sales	$2,000,000	$3,000,000
– *Marketing Costs*	$1,000,000	$2,000,000
Brand Value	$1,000,000	$1,000,000
Operating Margin	$1,000,000	$1,000,000
÷ Marketing Costs	$1,000,000	$2,000,000
Return on Marketing Costs	1.0	.5

CASE 2	Company A	Company B
Total Sales	$2,000,000	$1,250,000
– *Marketing Costs*	$1,000,000	$500,000
Brand Value	$1,000,000	$750,000
Operating Margin	$1,000,000	$750,000
÷ Marketing Costs	$1,000,000	$500,000
Return on Marketing Costs	1.0	1.5

The two cases are excellent and useful, if somewhat simple, illustrations of how measuring value only tells part of the brand equity story. While a strong brand can certainly return a premium value compared to competitors, it is even more helpful to know how efficient you are with the marketing investments that helped create the enhanced value in the first place.

Brand values may be similar, such as in Case 1, but the return on marketing costs indicates that Company A had a higher return on its marketing than Company B, indicating that it was more efficient with its marketing expenditures. In Case 2, Company A was less efficient with its marketing than Company B, even though A had a higher overall brand value. You can easily extrapolate that Company B is likely to overtake Company A in brand value one day if it continues with its marketing efficiencies.

The return on marketing costs is reflected by the formula:

$$\frac{V_b}{C_m}$$

Where

V_b = brand value
C_m = marketing costs

The return on marketing costs is based on brand value divided by marketing costs. Brand value is based on the difference between total revenues and total costs, and marketing efficiency measures the ratio of total revenues and total costs. Clearly, a higher ratio means the company has more efficient marketing and, consequently, this leads to higher brand equity. Marketing efficiency can be shown as:

$$\frac{R}{C_m}$$

Where

R = total revenues
C_m = marketing costs

To determine brand equity, therefore, brand value and marketing efficiency must be considered together. MacInnis and Park offer the following formula:

$$\frac{\text{Marketing Efficiency} \times \text{Total Revenues}}{1 + \text{Marketing Efficiency}}$$

Finally, MacInnis and Park mention that this analysis is useful if you are evaluating the same brand in the same industry. But if your objective is to compare the equity of your brand with that of another in a different industry, then they suggest adjusting the formula to reflect differing growth rates in each industry. The rationale is that growth rate differences between industries can distort brand-to-brand comparisons since one industry may be growing overall and, thereby, lifting the value of all companies within (a crude example would be the dot.com mania of the late 1990s), while a brand being compared from another industry may be affected by a slowdown in its industry (the U.S. auto industry, for example). In either case, individual brand equities are being distorted by the larger industry forces. Therefore, adjusting the formula by adding growth rates would be useful:

$$\frac{\text{Marketing Efficiency} \times \text{Total Revenues}}{1 + (1 + \text{growth rate}) \times \text{Marketing Efficiency}}$$

WHAT IT MEANS AND POTENTIAL CHALLENGES

MacInnis and Park's model provides an interesting approach, based on classic accounting techniques. It is useful as a method for calculating your brand equity using straightforward formulas and accessible company financial figures.

As with any model, the challenge is in determining the best possible estimates. In this case, calculating the marketing efficiency, or the ROI on marketing costs, is affected by a few not entirely controllable factors: the response of customers to a marketing communications effort; assumptions the company makes about its marketplace and its customers; and the reaction of competitors and how their strategies might impact on or even disrupt your plans. Given that brand equity often includes intangible factors, it is not possible to offer this conclusively as the best model of brand equity. As indicated by the various marketing experts at the beginning of this section, there are subtle differences in each definition. Nevertheless, they offer a worthwhile approach.

[1] Aaker, David A., *Building Strong Brands,* ©*1996 The Free Press*, p.319.
[2] MacInnis, Deborah; Park, C.W., "Making the Most of Your Brand: Leveraging Brand Equity Through Branding Strategies", March 2004, www.marketingprofs.com.

Brand–Name Premium

THE DEFINITION

From years of academic and industry research (and a bit of common sense), there is widespread agreement that a well-established brand-name can command higher prices over lesser-known rivals. If managed well, the ramifications of this for a business are impressive: improved profitability and a higher price-to-sales ratio. But how do you measure this?

THE FORMULA AND ITS COMPONENTS[1]

This is one of those "you are way over-thinking this" formulas, but the good news is it will keep CEOs and CFOs happy because it provides a reasonably fair measure of the value of a brand-name:

$$Vbn = \{(V/S)b - (V/S)g\} \times S$$

Where

Vbn   = value of brand-name
(V/S)b = value of company/sales ratio of the firm with the brand-name
(V/S)g = value of company/sales ratio of the firm with the generic product
S   = sales

WHERE'S THE DATA?

The data is quite easy to find in publicly traded companies. Simply refer to their published financial statements. For a privately held firm, you will need to identify the following information:

- pre-tax operating margin

- after-tax operating margin

- return on assets

- retention ratio

- expected growth

- costs of equity.

The figures used in the following example were taken from the Kellogg's 1994 financial statements. To determine the generic substitute's figures, data was gathered from a private-label cereal manufacturer. For firms based in Asia, generic and private-label data is harder to find. The private-label market in Asia is considerably smaller than in the U.S. or Europe, but it is also one of the fastest-growing markets for the category. Alternatively, manufacturers may produce and sell their own, unbranded products. Either way, the data about these products is still emerging and not as robust as it is in the U.S. and Europe. To acquire this data, a company should consider retaining a regional market-research firm to study the product and segment characteristics of the markets in which it wishes to operate.

CALCULATING IT

Example of Valuing a Brand-Name: Kellogg's

Here is an illustration in how to value a brand-name, using Kellogg's, the consumer-products company, as an example. This analysis is adapted from information at the NYU Stern School of Business website.

As mentioned above, the data for this analysis came from the 1994 financial statements. However, to complete the table below, we need to determine the expected growth in after-tax operating income. This equals:

Retention Ratio × Return on Assets

Therefore, the company's expected growth in after-tax income is as follows:

$.56 \times .326 = 18.26\%$

The expected growth in after-tax income for the private-label substitute is:

$$.56 \times .15 = 8.4\%$$

	Kellogg's	Private-label Substitute
Pre-tax Operating Margin	22.00%	10.50%
After-tax Operating Margin	14.08%	6.72%
Return on Assets	32.60%	15.00%
Retention Ratio	56.00%	56.00%
Expected Growth	18.26%	8.40%
Length of High Growth Period	5	5
Cost of Equity	13.00%	13.00%
E/(D + E)	92.16%	92.16%
D/(D + E)	8.50%	8.50%
Value/Sales Ratio	3.39	1.10

Using the formulas above, we can plug in the numbers from the chart:

Value of brand-name $= \{(V/S)b - (V/S)g\} \times$ Sales

$$= (3.39 - 1.10) \times (\$6.562 \text{ billion})$$

$$= \$15.026 \text{ billion}$$

Value of Kellogg's as a company $= 3.39\ (\$6.562 \text{ billion})$

$$= \$22.271 \text{ billion}$$

Using this analysis, the portion of Kellogg's value attributable to brand-name premium can be determined (approximately) as 67.5%:

$$\frac{\$15,026,000,000}{\$22,271,000,000} = 67.5\%$$

What it Means and Potential Challenges

Clearly, the value of a brand-name is substantial. Global companies work hard to promote their brand-names for the very simple reason that it allows them to establish mind-share (the space you occupy in the customers' mind vis-à-vis competitors),[2] charge higher prices than less well-known competitors, increase profitability, increase the price-to-sales ratio, and improve the overall value of the enterprise. The alert reader will note that brand equity comes to mind when mentioning the value of the enterprise. A high brand-name premium logically implies a high brand equity overall. As you will see in Magic Number 34, which discusses price premiums, the three concepts are closely related. What is less clear is how companies develop brand-names, earn trust from customers and sustain premium returns over the long term. It is not that these accomplishments are mysterious, because there are plenty of business books, seminars and real-world examples of how to do these things, but that they often differ in actual practice and execution from company to company, even within the same industry. I regularly get questions from my students at the undergraduate, graduate and executive-education levels that ask what the one or two key marketing formulas and frameworks are that can be applied in almost any situation. And I repeat the same answer each time: there isn't one universal law that applies equally to all situations. Each business adapts its efforts to develop a brand-name to its unique practices, competencies and the unpredictable responses from customers. Yet time and again, students find this frustrating. I can understand, to an extent. After all, we are regularly bombarded with pressure to measure everything and conclude that if it can't be measured it isn't worth doing. Practically speaking, that point of view is naive and even lazy. It undermines the years of effort, both successes and failures, which companies undertake in their often random walk toward becoming a recognized brand-name. It also fails to consider that customers, whether consumers or businesses, are governed as much by emotion as they are by reason and, therefore, even the most rational analysis can often be overturned by an impassioned plea or argument that captures the spirit and momentum of anticipated events, even if the data doesn't. The Kellogg's example sheds a bit more light on an inherently intangible asset, but it still does not offer a completely satisfying description of what that 67% really is, beyond a recognized name. Nevertheless, it is a reasonable starting point.

There are two ways to measure the awareness level in the market for your brand: recall and recognition. These will be described in the next two Magic Numbers.

[1] NYU Stern School of Business http://pages.stern.nyu.edu/~adamodar/New_Home_Page/lectures/brand.html.

[2] Alternatively, mind-share can be defined as: "The percentage of customers who named the competitor in responding to the statement 'Name the first company that comes to mind in this industry'." Source: Kotler, Philip; Ang Swee Hoon; Leong Siew Meng; Tan Chin Tiong, *Marketing Management: An Asian Perspective* p.236, Prentice Hall, ©2003.

Recall

The Definition

Recall can be a test of overall brand awareness or of advertising impact. In brand awareness, recall refers to a situation where, given a product category, a consumer can name (or recall) a brand without further prompting. This level of awareness can suggest that a reasonably strong brand has been built over time.

There are two types of recall, which are easily measured with recall tests. Consumers are asked which brands in a particular product class (e.g. soaps) they recall, and their replies tend to fall into one of the next two categories (and sometimes both):

- Top of mind: the first brand recalled

- Dominance: the only brand recalled.

In advertising, recall has a similar meaning, except that the consumer recall is triggered by reference to a particular media vehicle (television, radio, internet, print…) within a predetermined time after the ad has run or been shown. In this case, consumers are asked to recall advertising they have seen or heard in a given media vehicle. Within advertising recall are two variations: aided recall, where some of the ad's elements are described without mentioning the product or company; and unaided recall, where no prompting occurs.

The Formula and its Components

Recall is not a formula, but a question. Here are some examples (not exhaustive):

- *Which brands in this product class do you recall?*

- *Please describe the most memorable ad from the last television show you watched.*

- *Do you recall an ad that had trumpet music and birds flying?*

WHERE'S THE DATA?

Recall data is gathered through several different research techniques such as surveys, focus groups and interviews. The techniques can be conducted by an independent third-party market-research firm, or through your own, in-house research project. In either case, survey design is important as the way that questions are asked can affect how consumers answer. Focus groups must also be planned thoughtfully and led by an expert facilitator who can keep the discussion going and on track.

CALCULATING IT

Much of the information gathered from these research techniques is qualitative and, therefore, harder to quantify. However, a good market researcher or marketing manager would, at a minimum, summarize the findings overall, then organize the answers into common themes. Repeated comments can then be tallied to indicate which consumer insights are most common and which are marginal or irrelevant.

WHAT IT MEANS AND POTENTIAL CHALLENGES

Qualitative research, indeed even some quantitative research, is subject to bias and interpretation. That may sound discouraging to those of you seeking absolute answers from your marketing. If so, then you need to adjust your expectations. Recall is a reasonable test of how successful your marketing efforts have been to build awareness. But an important question to remember is "What period of time are you evaluating?" You may launch a marketing campaign and sales increase 25%. You may conclude from this that your campaign was the reason for the increase. But you might be wrong. The competition might have made a strategic blunder, causing customers to switch to your company. Or the marketing efforts of previous years might finally be bearing fruit, in which case, your predecessors deserve at least some of the credit. So how will you know? The answer is: you won't, at least not perfectly.

Recall can also be the proverbial double-edged sword if your product becomes so popular that it is increasingly viewed as generic. Here are some familiar examples of companies and/or products whose names have entered our mainstream vocabulary as generic categories incorporating all products of that type.

- FedEx

- Rollerblade

- Windsurfer

- Aspirin

- Cellophane

- Kleenex

- Escalator

- Xerox.

Recall can also result from a negative association, which means your product and/or company is at risk for being perceived poorly. Such associations can arise from:

- A bad meal at a restaurant

- Bad service at a hotel

- Poor customer service when returning a product

- Product performance not meeting expectations.

Companies risk developing negative recall results if their products or product associations (the extended touch points in the market where their product is represented) are controversial or offensive. Benetton has for years run advertising campaigns that tackle sensitive social issues in a direct, almost confrontational way, virtually daring consumers to use their products despite their bold messages. Nike, too, has regularly courted controversy with its athlete endorsements and outsourcing practices.

Recall can even affect entire industries. Prior to April 2000, it was considered glamorous to be working for a dot.com, irrespective of what it did or whether it actually made money. In the post-April 2000 world, dot.coms are often derided and labeled as the poster child of immature, poor businesses with bad planning and arrogant entrepreneurs. Thus, while recall of dot.coms is quite high, it is not the sort of recall one would wish, unless you prefer being remembered for the wrong or less-successful things you have done.

Recognition

THE DEFINITION

This refers to the awareness of a brand, product or advertisement once it has been mentioned by name and/or described.

THE FORMULA AND ITS COMPONENTS

See Magic Number 22 for a description. Recognition utilizes similar questions to understand the consumer's awareness. In effect, recognition research asks, *Have you been exposed to this brand before?*

WHERE'S THE DATA?

See Magic Number 22 for research techniques.

CALCULATING IT

See Magic Number 22 for how to evaluate the research results.

WHAT IT MEANS AND POTENTIAL CHALLENGES

The benefit of recognition is that it can reveal whether or not your advertising efforts are being recognized in the market. However, recognition is really the weaker cousin of recall since it requires that the consumer be prompted *directly* with the name of the company, product or a description of the literal advertising message.

RECOGNITION AND RECALL SUMMARY

High recognition and low recall is bad because it means consumers only remember you when prompted. High recall is better. But high recognition and high recall is best. Niche brands tend to have high recall with loyal consumers, but low overall recall and recognition in the general market. The combination of high recall and high recognition can often result in positive feelings with consumers. Familiarity often leads to success and premium perceptions over less-known rivals in both advertising and product perception. Of course, familiarity can also breed contempt, as cautioned in the recall description above. Finally, since part of the reason companies market is to build trust with consumers, their efforts to advertise and, thereby, attract attention often signal that they believe in their products and are willing to stand by them in public. At least, one hopes that is the case.

A key question you may be asking is "What is a good level of recall and recognition?" Since both are components of awareness, let's simply look at them in this context. Is an awareness level of 30% good or bad? The answer depends entirely on product and industry. For example, if you are a consumer-products company which is crowded with brand names, then it is conceivable that a 30% awareness is low vis-à-vis the competition. Of course, that is still a bit vague, so let's look at a specific category: laundry detergent.

Tide, from Procter and Gamble, is well known in most parts of the world. It is the category leader, and has been for years. In asking consumers if they can name a laundry detergent brand, Tide is likely to be one of several brands mentioned. Alternatively, if you were to ask consumers if they have heard of Tide, the likelihood of "Yes" being the answer is also quite high. Both indicate a high level of awareness. What is that level? Let's assume that it is 90%, which, crudely speaking, would mean that Tide is mentioned nine out of 10 times in surveys that ask respondents if they can name a brand of laundry detergent (recall) or if they remember the brand called Tide (recognition). If, however, you are a competitor and your awareness is 30% in this category, then clearly you are cited and remembered less than Tide. So, is 30% good? Compared to Tide, it is clearly not as good. Is 30% bad, in this case? Perhaps "bad" is an overstatement. Maddeningly, this is somewhat specific to the context. When compared to Tide, this other brand, called "X", does not generate the same level of awareness.

Let's look at this another way. If X had been launched in the past year or two, then a 30% awareness may signal a rapid rise and, conceivably, that Tide might have cause for concern from such a rapidly growing upstart. On the other hand, if X had been around as long as Tide, then its 30% awareness level would indicate that it is perceived as a distant competitor, far behind the leader.

This example is based on only one industry and one product category. Awareness in a niche market may be entirely different. A 30% rating could signal a strong, market-leading competitor in this instance. The point is that measuring awareness is more complex than a simple measure of recall and recognition. The next question once those metrics are known is "Compared to what?" And from there, you would want to determine if the awareness and comparison are consistent for your industry, extraordinary, or underwhelming. Therefore, it is important to look at awareness from a more in-depth perspective before deciding if yours is good, bad or indifferent.

MAGIC NUM8ER

24 Brand–Culture Framework

THE DEFINITION

Brand-culture is a framework for evaluating the talent inside your organization, the value of the corporate social culture (mores, values, traditions, unique practices) and the value of the programs used to train and develop people. This is a very fuzzy definition and, by its very nature, it is quite hard to assess with hard numbers. (How do you value Sheila down the hall? Purely on the basis of the salary you pay her? What about her contributions? How do you attach a value to her positive and constructive comments that inspire innovation?) Most importantly, brand-culture is a Magic Number because it is a vital driver in a firm's marketing success. The reason for this is simple: if the people inside an organization understand its products, marketing offers and customers, they are far more capable of helping the company deliver on its promises to the market effectively and successfully. Without a strong culture, marketing is an exercise in external communication that has no substance or credibility. As you read this, you may be thinking, "Oh come on, isn't marketing essentially composed of the 4Ps[1] and not this holistic 'everything is marketing' nonsense?" The short answer is, of course, "No". The 4Ps, and similar marketing frameworks such as the 5Cs,[2] are tools that help organize basic marketing components. But without the substance that comes from a supportive corporate culture, marketing is merely the proverbial slogans, logos and ads…external messages that are relatively meaningless — an empty promise.

THE FRAMEWORK AND ITS COMPONENTS

There is no formula for brand-culture, but there are four components that help companies understand how to create marketing value from a strong culture. When conducting an audit focusing on brand-culture, a series of questions designed to elicit insights about subjective performance behaviors are asked. These are captured in a culture scorecard that management can use to understand better how their employees work and identify possible performance gaps. The scorecard would incorporate the following four components, each of which is considered in detail below:

- Talent Measures — People
- Behavior Measures — Five Ambassadors
- Team — Organization
- Performance Measures — Social Fabric.

Talent Measures — People

Without a doubt, developing and nurturing a vibrant corporate culture requires attracting and developing the best people. Within this measure are several additional determinants of success.

Talent Acquisition and Retention

Attracting the right people with the right skills and the right personality is obviously HR 101. Marketing is introducing nothing new here nor laying claim to a profound insight. However, by recognizing that a strong culture can help a brand succeed, it puts a sizable responsibility on the company and its hiring managers to try to do this right. Not every hire is going to be a perfect match. But in this day and age, we are past hiring people to be "slot-fillers" because much of the developed world's economic success is owed to brain-work, not brawn-work. When a company truly understands that its people represent the company, even if their job does not put them in direct contact with the customer or the market on a regular basis, then it has set an expectation that it wants people who are a good match with the company's overall objectives. Furthermore, retention is the necessary next step in the talent-management process. Thus, both the hiring and retaining of the best talent is a responsibility that the company owes to its products, its brand, its reputation and its customers.

Training

Retention is partly influenced by the ongoing training (and commitment to training) that a firm has for its talent. Training is more than merely basic skills work, although for entry-level talent, it is certainly a reasonable offering. Training is the organization's commitment to ensuring that its most promising rising stars get the proper support and education to not only further their knowledge, but contribute to the successful growth and value of the enterprise for the long term. It is an investment in offering training that is relevant to employees at different stages in their careers. And it is expensive. At the risk of being dramatic, however, the greater expense is often associated with ignoring the education needs of employees. Training is not merely focused on skills or business fundamentals. It also embodies team-building events, company culture-building activities and story telling, and definitely includes showing employees each and every new product, marketing campaign, sales promotion, customer information, competitor insights and so forth. After all, by providing this information, firms have a much greater chance of developing inspired, passionate employees who become believers in the company's offerings, its values and its ultimate destiny.

Transition and Succession

Attracting the right talent and providing them with the right training is done to help prepare employees for the next stage in their career. Typically, these stages are either a transition to a parallel job but a new responsibility, or a promotion to a more complex role with greater authority. Thus, the right talent with the right education will hopefully become the organization's right leaders for the future. The value the market places on a company's succession planning is most evidenced by publicly traded firms such as GE and Disney.

- **GE and Disney**

GE, particularly under Jack Welch, was dedicated to grooming talented people to run challenging businesses in complex industries against formidable competitors. When Jack Welch succeed Reg Jones and when Jeff Immelt succeeded Jack Welch, it was quite apparent that customers and Wall Street paid close attention to these transitions. GE made it a public, transparent effort, not only to let the market know that it was on top of important strategic issues like leadership, but also to let the "candidates" for the CEO position know that they were being evaluated not behind closed doors, but in full view of the market that would ultimately judge them. This was daunting to the candidates, perhaps, but it reassured customers and the market that GE was interested in only the best leaders.

Disney, on the other hand, has suffered in the past few years from Michael Eisner's unclear succession plans (that is, until he finally announced in Spring 2004 his departure upon the conclusion of his employment contract, no doubt influenced by dissident shareholders, an increasingly frustrated Wall Street and a financial performance in recent years that can be described as flat. Since then, he has named Robert Iger, a long-time Disney executive, as his successor). Eisner's first decade or so was generally considered a tremendous success. But the death of Frank Wells, Disney's #2 executive, in the early 1990s revealed the importance of having a strong leadership TEAM (not just a strong individual leader) to an organization's success.

GE's performance during Jack Welch's second decade as CEO was stronger than Eisner's at Disney, and part of this is due to the favorable perception and confidence the market had in GE's succession plans. In fact, the market's confidence was not just in the CEO succession plans, but a widely acknowledged deep talent pool GE had in most divisions throughout the company. This was further reinforced over the years by the number of GE executives who have gone on to run other large companies successfully.

Why mention these in relation to marketing? Because part of marketing's role is to create value that attracts customers and grows the business profitably. Having the right talent at all levels can contribute directly to the overall market capitalization of the enterprise. As we discussed regarding brand value, well-known and respected brands command premium market value and profits over their lesser-known rivals. The value of talent is a necessary ingredient to this marketing equation.

Behavior Measures — Five Ambassadors

The Five Ambassadors is an individual-performance framework I have been developing to describe the behaviors of top performers. It is the result of interviews with 15 CEOs of U.S. companies and media leaders; reviews of top sales performers in three industries: hospitality, consumer products and enterprise software; and student research of over 50 companies in the U.S. and Asia. Each of the Five Ambassadors is a specific behavior exhibited by the top performers at different times of their job. Typically, these behaviors were most prominent when the individual was either selling a product, service or idea. The top performer gracefully shifted from one Ambassador role to the next, depending on the response of the buyer. The Five Ambassadors were also exhibited if the top performers were seeking something (funding, budget increase, assistance on a project) from another party. It is important to understand that these behaviors are rarely conscious. In other words, the top performer did not think to him or herself, "Now I must act like a resource ambassador." Rather, the Five Ambassadors were a fluid set of behaviors that ultimately convinced the other party of the merits of the top performer's argument. Each of the Five Ambassadors encompasses multiple behaviors within, but the behaviors were similar enough to be grouped into the broader Ambassador designations. Separately, each of the Five Ambassadors is an admirable set of behavior characteristics. But collectively, they are a powerful combination of skills that contributes to the overall success of the enterprise.

Brand Ambassador

This describes an individual's efforts to present their company, product or department to another person or group (customer, vendor or another internal department), using visual or verbal imagery. Visual imagery is self-explanatory: top performers are adept at using relevant visual examples to complement their presentation, making it memorable and connecting the audience to the initiative being presented. Verbal imagery deals with the words used to paint verbal pictures. It is easy to blather on and on and much harder to get to the point succinctly and clearly (in the words of Mark Twain, "I didn't have time to write you a short letter, so I wrote you a long one.").

- **Scott Bedbury**

Scott Bedbury, who was Nike's former VP of Advertising, Starbucks' VP of Worldwide Marketing, the author of *A New Brand World*, and a guest lecturer in my courses at the University of Washington, is a master of this. He has the ability to capture the imagination of his audience (whether one or many) through his use of words and images, draw them into his "world", and have them leave the room utterly convinced that whatever he said was right. I saw this several times at Nike when Scott would launch the new ad campaigns. He wouldn't just say, "Here's the new ad for Air Whatever". Instead, he would describe the creative process that led to the completed ad, show some of the rejects and finally set up the new ad by showing images of the target audience, why they would respond and whether it "moved the needle", as he used to say. Nike sales reps and retailers couldn't wait to see the finished ads, partly because they knew the ads came with their own unique history. This history got the audience more involved and interested in the finished product. By the time they had left the presentation, they almost felt as if they had directed the ads themselves.

More recently, I invited Scott to be a guest lecturer in my Strategic Marketing course in the EMBA program at the University of Washington. My graduate students, most of whom were senior executives and all seasoned professionals, saw Scott give a preview for his book *A New Brand World*. He showed Nike ads, told Starbucks stories and shared his uniquely passionate perspective on how to build brands. Over the years, Scott has used a thoughtful combination of verbal and visual imagery to convey his message. The bottom line is that the brand ambassador behaviors contribute significantly toward creating a favorable image and perception of a company and its products. This, in turn, enhances the value of the enterprise through market capitalization, increased customer loyalty, and generating awareness that creates a cycle of buzz that promotes the company.

Resource Ambassador

This set of behaviors describes the top performer's understanding of his or her own company. This is not merely a surface-level awareness of the company's products, but an in-depth understanding of their own organization, who was most influential, how different departments contribute, and which resources would be most appealing and relevant to the buying or receiving party. It is often exhibited as an explicit description of which departments or functions were part of the solution being sold. For example, in the enterprise-software industry, a product sale is far more than just the software. It includes engineering support, customer service, warranties, consulting and so on. Once the sale is made, the customer is quite interested in making sure the product functions as specified and, if not, what remedies are available. Top performers understand this and in the pre-sales effort they work hard to describe these various resources to convince the customer that the company supports its products and to differentiate themselves from competing products. Another example is in an internal or intra-organizational effort, such as when a project manager is working to persuade a colleague in another department to be part of a new project, even though this may not fall within the colleague's main responsibilities. Thus, the colleague needs to understand the project and why his or her services are needed and, furthermore, how it benefits the department and company. The bottom line is that the resource ambassador behaviors connect a company to the customer beyond the core product purchase by extending the product definition to include the areas that support it. As a result, the customer develops confidence that the company will support the products it sells.

- **Ron Hill**

Ron Hill was one of my key bosses during my tenure at Nike. At the time, he was Global Merchandise Director for Footwear, which meant he was responsible for ensuring that Nike's various footwear product lines (basketball, tennis, track, baseball, soccer, cross training…) had enough diversity and uniqueness to make them into a compelling merchandise mix. In effect, he had the power to tell marketing managers, who ran their product categories, which shoes could and should be in the product line, and which should be dropped. Prior to this, Ron had been in charge of the basketball category, helping it grow to global market dominance. Ron knew footwear. Before he came to Nike, he had been with Nordstrom, one of the foremost upscale retail department store chains in the U.S. If anybody knew merchandising, it was Ron. But that was not what made him successful.

Ron's gift was internal know-how. He knew which departments, indeed which people in each department, were critical to getting a job done. Furthermore, he knew how to get people from different divisions to work together on projects, a hard thing to do when you realize that those other departments are compensated for entirely different performance targets. Ron was able to recommend who should be brought on board to pursue a given initiative. Furthermore, he knew how to communicate to each person he sought, convincing them of their importance to the task required. However, once those various resources had been assembled into a team (for example, a sales analyst, a retail marketing associate, a marketing manager, a developer, a sales rep, a finance person…), he then presented that team as a unified whole to the target audience. If the target audience was a retail customer, then Ron would tell that customer about the strengths of the people on the team and why they benefited the retailer. As obvious as that sounds, it is rare to see this consistently exhibited in an organization. Inside Nike, Ron's resource efforts created alliances so that different departments could come together to accomplish a significant task. Outside, his efforts could convince retailers that the team really understood a particular sports category, compelling them to increase their orders, merely because they perceived the Nike team as more competent. In both instances, knowledge of one's own resources, how to use them and inspire them, is a critical step in strengthening a firm's business performance. While quantifying it is quite hard, few of us would argue that this approach offers more benefits than risks.

Knowledge Ambassador

As the title implies, the Knowledge Ambassador reflects the knowledge that the top performer has and uses to describe for the buyer or recipient conditions in the market with competitors, trends in the economic environment and other similar information. As most of us are aware, there is a seemingly endless stream of distractions and activities that consume much of our daily work. So much so that it is hard to step back and look at the broader market and business conditions to see what threats and opportunities may be emerging. Consequently, top performers work hard to learn about the rest of the market and the factors that could eventually affect the customer's business. The top performer then presents this information throughout the sales or persuasion process to help the customer understand outside conditions and influences that could affect their business (hence the "need" to buy the product). This knowledge is gleaned from a wide range of sources (the Internet, magazines, newspapers…) and becomes a crucial aspect of the top performer's efforts to win the customer. The Knowledge Ambassador behaviors are ongoing, usually because the effort to win a customer takes more than one meeting. It takes many meetings, calls, letters and delays. Top performers frequently update their market knowledge so that they can be an advocate for both the customer and their own company while demonstrating why the customer needs their products to be successful in the challenging environment described. The bottom line is that the Knowledge Ambassador behaviors help the customer become smarter about their own business and why the seller's products are an integral piece of the customer's success. The seller provides market insight on the customer's customers, competitors and economic trends that might affect their business in the future. For the seller, this knowledge creates a deeper bond with the customer than a more traditional arms-length transaction, which helps support the next Ambassador role.

- **David Lowe**

David Lowe is a former colleague who worked on my marketing team at Transamerica Intellitech, one of Transamerica Corporation's real-estate companies. Transamerica Intellitech was in the data business, offering information on U.S. residential real estate, along with software that accessed the data, to four core customer groups: real-estate companies, title companies, appraisers and mortgage firms.

David started out in the company as a communications writer, but his aptitude and energy were apparent. As I was building my team, which included product managers, web designers and market researchers, it was clear that we needed somebody who could craft marketing communications that were to the point, yet also relevant to the market. These communications included print ads, trade show activities, early on-line efforts (including an intranet), as well as a more consistent company brand identity. David was young, only 26, but he was sharp and eager. Plus, he had the ability to learn quickly and communicate clearly. However, his greatest asset was his ability to learn and quickly absorb a range of business, market and industry information and translate it into useful information for the rest of the company. This was exemplified by his successful efforts to build the company's first intranet. Keep in mind that this was late 1996 and early 1997, when intranets were still a relatively unknown idea. David worked with our new team of marketing researchers to aggregate customer and competitor data over several weeks and organize it into an easy-to-use intranet that offered extensive information regarding all of our customers and key competitors. This was information that was previously known only to each individual sales rep, who then only knew his or her individual accounts and not those of their colleagues in their territory or even other markets. Furthermore, the intranet revealed information about competitors, including overviews of their products, known customers and pricing…again, all available to employees of the company. Transamerica Intellitech had over 400 employees at this time, who were now a far more informed and potentially powerful corporate asset, simply because they had a better sense about the market.

But David did not stop there. He was also a relentless communicator, sharing knowledge with headquarters employees through regular presentations. Furthermore, he traveled with sales reps and also spent a significant amount of time on the phone with them to provide them with the latest research and to glean recent insights from them about conditions on their respective territories. David also surveyed customers regularly, in cooperation with our market research team, to learn what they liked and disliked about our products, but also to learn what they would like to see us do in the future. He would meet regularly with each of the category marketing managers, each of whom was responsible for a product line, and provide them with relevant insights about their target customers, which allowed us to create better and more appropriate products to fit their needs. David's tireless efforts promulgated important knowledge to our employees and our customers that enabled Transamerica Intellitech to be a more effective and successful competitor in what was then a highly fragmented national industry, with dozens of players but only two or three truly national players, of which it was one.

Relationship Ambassador

Business, in many ways, is about relationships before it is about profits. Who you know often determines whether you will be successful. Do you know your customers? Do you know the key buyers? Do you know them well? Do you understand how they make decisions? The Relationship Ambassador behaviors describe how sellers relate to buyers. In a consumer-products context, a sales rep for a packaged-goods company must have a deep understanding of the retail buyers. Not just the company, but the buyers. And not just their names, but who they are, what they like and hate, what their interests are, why they have bought before, what they have bought before and a host of similar issues. Getting to know your customer is becoming increasingly personal. It includes the subtler, fuzzier things such as even knowing their birthdays and anniversaries so that the seller can continue to stay in touch. Furthermore, the Relationship Ambassador behaviors continue even when a sale has been completed. In this regard, the seller nurtures the buyer, staying in touch informally and formally to ensure that the product is working well. The reason for this is apparent: even though another sale may not be on the near-term horizon, the seller wants to be the first person the buyer thinks of when it comes time to purchase again. Therefore, developing the relationship beyond the sale is crucial.

- **Don Skloss**

For example, Don Skloss is a career sales executive living in the Pacific Northwest of the U.S. He has been in sales management at the field and executive levels most of his career. He has been in both the consumer-products industry with companies like Johnson & Johnson, Resers, Dean Foods and Kraft, and has also worked in real estate and digital data with Transamerica Intellitech and TerraPointe. Don has sold successfully and directly to accounts and he has managed national sales forces as well. In all cases, he has worked closely with customers, whether it was WalMart in Arkansas or the California Association of Realtors. In working with customers, Don knows that a sale is not a one-time event, but a lifetime opportunity. During his 20-year career to date, he has developed a network of customers in multiple industries. But it is more than a network. He has developed relationships and friendships. These customers know Don, trust him and are supported by him, even when a sale is not imminent. He knows how to work with large, strategic accounts by including key reps from his sales force to ensure the customer is happy. And he knows how to work with smaller customers, by offering them individualized one-on-one service. In both cases, his focus is on the customer and his or her needs. Like many supremely successful sales people, Don does this for two reasons: he loves selling and he loves working with people.

- **Tom Phillips**

Another example of Relationship Ambassador behaviors can also be found internally, that is, inside your own organization. Large consumer-products companies like Nike, P&G, Nestlé, Clorox, Kao, and Samsung regularly develop a steady stream of new products. It takes a well-coordinated effort among managers in different departments to make new products happen. Often, the managers work in cross-functional teams where the team leader is not the boss of the others on the team. Each team member in these instances is from a different department and each has individual departmental responsibilities. The challenge as a team leader is to keep the team on track and inspire the members to contribute. At Nike, each product group, from running to cross-training to tennis, typically comprises three core functions: a marketing or product manager, a development manager and a designer. The marketing manager is responsible for understanding the general customer market and business conditions, developing the product line plan, setting target prices and selling his or her team on the next season's set of new products. The development manager is responsible for sourcing materials and factories and is quite concerned with making the product cost-effectively and efficiently. The designer is tasked with taking the marketing manager's words and translating them into commercial designs. The challenge is getting all three functions to work together toward a common objective because the marketers are looking at the overall business, the developers are focused primarily on costs and the designers are thinking about creating new products. Developers and designers may not always agree with the marketer's assessment of the market and the needs of the target customers; marketers may see the designer's creations as too extreme to be appealing; and developers may think that neither the marketer's financial objectives (price point, for example) nor the designer's creations are feasible.

Tom Phillips was once Marketing Manager in charge of Nike's Kids division. I got to know him when I was Marketing Manager for ACG (All Conditions Gear, the outdoor products group). When I first met Tom, he had already been with Nike for seven years and was wise in the ways of building internal relationships. I had just finished graduate school and was quite green when it came to doing things the Nike way. My first couple of seasons managing a team were rough. My team constantly fought with me over customer profiles, product direction and general market understanding. Yet whenever I saw Tom, his team appeared to be harmonious and he was constantly smiling and getting the products he wanted. Watching Tom in action revealed some key insights: First, he took on the persona of a kid in everything he did. His office was littered with toys, posters and videos. Second, he was never unhappy, or if he was he never projected it to his team or his colleagues. He exhibited child-like astonishment at the wonders of the world and regularly used a kid's point of view whenever he discussed his product line. Third, he knew what inspired his team. He knew what his teammates loved outside of work, whether it was cars or gardening or skiing. He knew his teammates' families and what toys their children played with. And whenever he presented to his teams his ideas for a new season of products, he wove this knowledge directly into his team meetings. When speaking of customers, he wouldn't use the typical demographic breakdowns. Instead, he would describe the customer in terms that reflected the passions of his teammates (if a team member loved cars, he would describe the target customer as a "miniature Red Ferrari, eager to race past his friends..."; or, if a team mate loved gardening, he would describe the product as a "brilliant tropical flower with an amazing fragrance..."). Consequently, his teammates embraced Tom's ideas because he had communicated with them personally. This implies something quite important: Tom worked exceedingly hard to build relationships with his teammates. He took them out to dinners, bought them cool gifts for birthdays and holidays, held team meetings in unusual off-site locations, took his team to toy trade shows and kids' sporting events. He constantly wandered the hallways at Nike, talking to his teammates, to colleagues, to ANYBODY. He was visible, sincere, fun and energetic and this further demonstrated to his team that he loved the business and was serious about it as well. It was not calculating — it was genuine love of the products, the market, his team and the business overall and his teammates sensed it and believed it. The bottom line is that the Relationship Ambassador behaviors enable people to develop a strong bond with customers and colleagues, creating mutual dependencies that make it easier for business to be conducted because everyone knows each other so well. Without a doubt, this contributes to direct financial success, yet it is hard to pinpoint a specific number or formula.

Experience Ambassador

Modifying a quote from Vince Lombardi, a famous former head coach in the U.S. National Football League, "Top performers are made, not born. Their efforts are the result of rich experiences that combine success and failure, influencing their successes today." Thus, the Experience Ambassador behaviors relate to the wisdom that comes from trial and error and the application of that wisdom everyday.

- **Jack Crawford**

Jack Crawford is the founder and Managing Director of Capital Valley Ventures (CVV), a California-based firm which specializes in early-stage funding for young high-tech companies. Jack founded CVV in 2001 when he saw an opportunity…an apparently counter-intuitive opportunity. The high-tech market had melted down, leaving many established venture capital (VC) firms holding hundreds of millions of dollars of investors' money with no outlet for investment because of the spectacular flame-out of so many start-up companies from the late 1990s. As these VCs shifted their business model toward more established firms by providing mezzanine and pre-IPO capital, a void developed for the pure start-up. Jack saw his opportunity and started CVV as a result. Since 2001, CVV has built a multi-million-dollar fund that has invested in numerous innovative companies in the biotech and high-tech sectors. Prior to CVV, Jack had started four technology companies and had shepherded them through the extreme ups and downs that a start-up regularly faces. Ultimately, most of these firms were sold or were merged into larger entities and Jack's experiences gave him both the credibility and reputation that he knew what he was doing. This was vital in the early stages of CVV since founding a VC company is substantially different than founding a high-tech firm. His knowledge gained from the experience of working with VCs and angel investors[3] on behalf of his previous companies exposed him to how VCs think and operate, and he felt he could build from that experience by creating an updated VC company. His experience included building a strong network of senior executives and entrepreneurs in high-tech with whom he regularly shared ideas. These high-level business contacts, in turn, served to recommend key partners for CVV as it built its business.

While Jack understands technology companies, his real strength is people. He knows how to attract the right people and develop the right contacts. He has built a credible reputation and another successful business. CVV would have been a far greater challenge had Jack not had the experience working in extremely challenging business conditions through several start-ups. The bottom line is that the Experience Ambassador behaviors are not built overnight. This may explain why many of the dot.com companies ultimately failed — not enough experience at the senior level. Top performers like Jack recognize that excellence comes with substantial hard work, extraordinary challenges and learning how to be resilient in tough times.

Overall, the Five Ambassadors are a seamless pattern of behaviors exhibited by top performers. However, I do not want to mislead you into thinking that the people discussed in this section were perfect or excellent 100% of the time. They themselves would admit this because a key characteristic of the top performers studied is humility. They never felt that they had all the answers and they regularly credited those with whom they worked in their efforts. Top performers exhibit an innate sense of who can help them and how to inspire those people to work with them toward a common goal. Furthermore, the Five Ambassadors are behaviors that *tend* to come out when the pressure is really on. Rather than approaching each business relationship with a methodical, rigid plan outlining their behavior, the top performers combine spontaneity with thoughtful planning to achieve their objectives.

The Five Ambassadors model is designed as a qualitative model. The behaviors affect performance measures across the company. Having taught this model the past three years in EMBA and executive-education programs, I've found that the reactions from students vary from "It perfectly captures the qualities I want my team to have" to "I agree with it, but how can it be described formulaically?" The benefits to an organization are immense, however, because the Five Ambassadors describes the behavior of truly top performers — people who have built or led companies, or have achieved extraordinary performance levels in sales or project management (new product launches, for example) — and their lessons are both admirable and imitable.

During my career I have been assessed or have evaluated people who work for me on a combination of qualitative and quantitative performance factors. Measurable targets are often called "MBOs", "Management By Objectives", meaning that one has certain financial targets to achieve to earn a bonus or promotion or some other form of recognition. However, while some who worked for me sometimes fell short in achieving their MBOs, the full bonus was still given because of the other performance measures — the qualitative measures which answered questions such as:

- Did they contribute above and beyond the call of duty?

- Did they identify new opportunities or threats not previously known?

- Did they attract new talent into the organization?

- Did they inspire their team AND other internal teams to exceed expectations?

- Did they represent the very highest ideals?

These qualitative measures have a powerful impact on the psyche of an organization, one that is akin to the person who walks into a room and immediately the entire dynamic of the room changes for the better. There is simply something about that person that inspires people to achieve what was thought to be unachievable. The Five Ambassadors, while not numerical measures, are behavioral measures. To understand their importance another way, let's look at a very common approach: measuring performance purely on measurable objectives.

Some people exceed MBOs by a wide margin, breaking sales records, creating new products or boosting market share over a key competitor. There are instances in which these high achievers did so at the expense of other people. In effect, they ran roughshod over colleagues, subordinates and even bosses in their quest to achieve. Yet by doing so, what have they really accomplished? While their numbers look good, their colleagues either quit, feel betrayed or have no incentive to offer support or assistance to aid this "superior performer". Ultimately, this person becomes isolated. While their performance may be great, they have left a trail of bitter colleagues, broken relationships and battered psyches in their wake. Short-term achievements like this rarely last long.

Clearly, a blend of the Five Ambassadors with a solid set of stretch quantitative targets is the ideal combination. But one without the other is rarely sustainable.

Performance Measures — Organization

As broad as it sounds, Organization is focused on the roles of people within. There are three primary roles people fulfill within an organization:

- Leaders
- Teams
- Individuals.

Leaders

The role of leaders in an organization's success has been studied for years. Different leadership models have been prescribed and they range from individual will to consensus management, from dictatorial to cooperative. Bill Gates' (and now Steve Balmer's) style as CEO of Microsoft is vastly different from that of Steve Jobs, yet no one would argue that both have been effective. Jobs' remarkable salesmanship and dynamic personality have continued to improve with time. Carly Fiorina was also considered to be a dynamic sales person, with qualities which initially served her well at HP, particularly in her efforts to acquire Compaq. Yet these same traits likely contributed to her downfall in early 2005 when she was asked to resign by HP's board. Sony's recent leadership transition from Nobuyuki Idei to Howard Stringer is both surprising and interesting. Idei enjoyed early success when he first became CEO in 1995 (with the launch of Sony PlayStation, the Vaio computer line and the turnaround of its movie studio led by Idei's handpicked team), earning a reputation for bold decision making and solid leadership. In the early 2000s, Sony then faltered, losing ground to Apple and

Samsung in the process. Idei chose Howard Stringer as his replacement in early 2005, the first non-Japanese to lead one of Japan's most respected companies. Stringer had proven himself as head of Sony's U.S. Operations, turning one success into another, including the movie and music businesses and a successful cost-cutting effort that surpassed the parent company's expectations. His style has been very different from Idei's.

Each of them exhibited behaviors and traits consistent with research about successful leaders. Each found success yet not all were able to sustain it. What is the common thread, the key leadership difference, the proverbial silver-bullet solution that tells us the right factors for successful leaders? While there is no single definition that provides this, the leaders I interviewed shared each of the Five Ambassadors qualities.

In addition, they exhibited the following six characteristics:

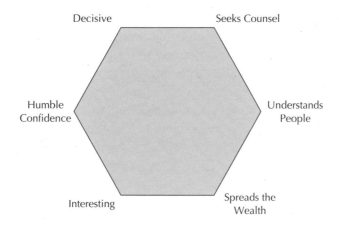

- They were interesting people who were interesting to be around.

- They understood people and took pleasure in talking to colleagues, junior staffers and employees at large.

- They did not build personal empires or kingdoms in which employees served the leader. Instead, they shared knowledge and successes so that the entire organization benefited. Gone are the days when knowledge was power and owned by a privileged few. Knowledge is power only when everyone within has access to it.

- They sought the advice of those who worked for them, knowing that they had built strong teams of experts. These leaders also recognized that they did not have all the answers, nor were they concerned if they did not know something, because they knew that someone in the organization did.

- These leaders had a refreshing combination of self-confidence and humility. They did not believe their own press, in other words. They knew their organizations would exist beyond their tenure and they therefore had a responsibility to lead it thoughtfully so that the next generation of leaders could continue to guide.

- They were decisive. While decision making has been analyzed, researched, evaluated, assessed, written about and preached for years, it was abundantly clear that these leaders did not shy away from making decisions. More often than not, they exhibited a bias toward action rather than delay for more information ("analysis paralysis", as it is often pejoratively termed). They felt it was better to make a decision now and deal with the repercussions tomorrow, than to wait and miss an opportunity. However, I want to be careful NOT to suggest that they were incautious or thrill-seeking risk-takers. This is where the Experience Ambassador comes into play because each of the leaders was comfortable making decisions because they had a rich and diverse background of making decisions for a variety of challenges. Each had a sense of what made them comfortable when considering a decision. They had grown accustomed to making decisions in the absence of complete information and, often, in circumstances of extreme ambiguity.

Not surprisingly, leadership is usually described in the context of an entity's main leader (President, CEO, Managing Director, Prime Minister…). A key point to this section is recognizing that the lessons these visible leaders provide is transferable to leaders *within* the organization. Leadership does include leading by example and the act of doing so can create a powerful organization that has a competitive advantage for a very key reason: even if competitors succeed at copying your products, it is quite hard to copy your organization. Instilling and inspiring a culture of leadership is an invaluable strategic asset that contributes to the value of the enterprise.

- **MAS Holdings**

In the Fall of 2004, I spent a few days visiting with the leaders and managers of MAS Holdings in Sri Lanka, along with a couple of colleagues from Singapore Management University. MAS Holdings is a manufacturer of apparel, working with an impressive list of global customers including Nike, Victoria's Secret, Lands' End, Banana Republic and Speedo. The name of the company is derived from the first names of the three brothers who started it in the mid 1980s, Mahesh, Ajay and Sharad Amalean. The company has since grown to approximately US$600 million in sales and was mentioned in *Fortune Magazine* in 2004 as the secret behind the success of Victoria's Secret. Meeting with the founders, managers and employees at the corporate office and at the factories reveals why MAS Holdings is so successful. From the top down, the people with whom we met were confident, inspiring and obviously devoted to the success of the company. They truly believed they worked for the best company on earth. This was as true for the line employees in manufacturing as it was for the three founding brothers. This is due partly to the leadership example set by the brothers, but it is reinforced through a corporate culture that is dedicated to being the best in product quality and having the best talent at every level.

The CEO is Mahesh Amalean, whom everyone agrees is the driving leader who sets the example. But meeting with his two brothers, Ajay and Sharad, reveals that each of them firmly believes that they have a responsibility to lead by example. Each has a different strength, but they are united toward a common goal and vision of making MAS the very best in its industry. They have established a common objective — called 1–1–10 — to be the "Number 1 preferred partner of the world's leading brands on intimates, sportswear and leisurewear with a turnover of US$1 billion by 2010". These goals have been translated to each division, department and individual so that everyone understands where their role fits in the organization and what they need to achieve individually to ensure the goal is achieved. Collectively, their leadership has enabled MAS to grow rapidly, earn customer loyalty, garner acclaim, and inspire the next layers of leaders below them.

Teams

Here again, MAS Holdings is different from many companies. From my own experience at Nike, I saw the power of a well-oiled team. This is not a revelation. But it is surprising how few companies embrace and nurture the team concept, despite saying the right things like "We believe in building great teams" or "The strength of our company lies in the collective effort of our teams". Yet these statements are often insufficiently supported or, worse, are not built into the performance measures for the organization or culture.

MAS Holdings believes in the power of teams. This is displayed time and again at the corporate and manufacturing facility level, where projects and performance goals are set for team accomplishments. MAS supports the team concept because it believes that employees gain far more from diverse points of view in overcoming challenges and arriving at innovative solutions. Borrowing from Jim Collins' book *Good To Great: Why Some Companies Make the Leap...And Others Don't*, Ajay Amalean said that a guiding philosophy was "getting the right people on the bus" and getting them to "work collaboratively". The reason is driven by its business model: MAS works with suppliers and customers often under a joint-venture structure, based on mutual trust. It wants to be known for being easy to do business with and for honoring commitments. In turn, it expects the same from its partners and employees.

For example, we visited the company's performance design operation, known as Linea MAS, and met with one of the group's marketing managers. The Linea MAS team works with many important clients, including Nike. The marketing manager we met was vibrant, articulate and focused. Two other members of the team met with us as well. All three echoed the same sentiments about MAS's strengths (starting with the leadership example set by the brothers), the importance of having unwavering commitment to their customers, creating cutting edge designs and executing flawlessly. None of this is achievable, they said, without a very strong commitment to team, both within MAS Holdings and with partners. As the marketing manager told us, "our number one asset is our credibility". While many companies state this, there is NO question that MAS Holdings and its employees believe it and execute it successfully. While the Linea MAS team is lean, with fewer than 45 people, it generates more than $75 million in revenue. Within this group, the design teams typically comprise five people and each team is focused on a single customer. Part of their success is due to their team philosophy, which is marketing-driven, not sales-focused.

They listen to the customer and create products based on customers' needs. Interestingly, this group has become so successful that it is increasingly designing its own leading-edge products as well. This would not have been possible in the early stages of building the business, but as time has progressed, its strong customer listening skills, excellent product quality and consistent results have enabled Linea MAS to develop credibility with its customers. Consequently, Linea MAS offers customers additional value with its design expertise. As we discovered, the marketing manager leads the team by example, just as the brothers lead the overall company in the same way.

Individuals

As individuals, everyone in an organization has the opportunity, indeed the responsibility, to represent the firm in the best possible light. There are really two choices: be world class or be mediocre. Howard Schultz, founder and CEO of Starbucks, once said his greatest fear is not failure but mediocrity. Each person can choose to work toward being world class, or can settle for uninspiring mediocrity.

Here, too, MAS Holdings offers a strong example of how individuals contribute to the strength of the enterprise. First, the company demonstrates the power of its belief in the individual by developing strong support programs designed to inspire people to achieve. A case in point is its "Women Go Beyond" campaign. The program is designed to recognize the achievements of top female performers in the company (more than 70% of the employees are female) and how they contributed. The award winners are recognized through ceremonial events internally and celebratory signage, posters and plaques highlighting their achievements. In the paternal corporate cultures often found throughout Asia, this type of recognition is unusual, progressive and powerful.

Deepthi de Silva is MAS Holdings' Group Director of Human Resources. In describing MAS's people philosophy and how it connects to performance measures, Deepthi was insistent that the company's success now and in the future is dependent on providing great jobs and paying people well for excellent performance. As he said, "If someone puts in a strong effort, they will earn strong rewards." Furthermore, he indicated that MAS employees must have an entrepreneurial spirit, since decisions must often be made even at the manufacturing line level.

Finally, he mentioned with pride that MAS provides "the very best training and education" for its employees. Each of these elements reinforces and fosters a "can-do" spirit at MAS. While this is intangible, it is also powerful and easily felt when one visits the company and its operations.

As Deepthi said, MAS wants people to take on responsibility, be curious and trust in one another. The company has certain specific expectations. Each employee needs to be in one of four competency levels in the company's performance criteria. These are progressive levels of performance and are designed to guide employees to achievement toward the next level. Each employee is responsible for setting his or her annual objectives, which are reviewed by his or her boss. If the objectives are met, a bonus is paid. Employees also get a company-wide bonus if the overall performance objectives of the company are met.

MAS's financial goals are communicated throughout the company. They look at ROE, ROI, on-time delivery, and efficiency-yields in plant operations to assess success, evaluate performance and uncover areas of need.

Throughout MAS, from executive to entry-level, from leader to individual and with teams, the company has articulated a very clear set of inspiring expectations and goals that everyone understands and is aligned behind.

Culture Measures — Social Fabric

Social Fabric describes how people work with each other in terms of custom, practice and tradition. This goes beyond performance measures and drills down into how values and practices are embedded deeply into the culture of the company.

- **Joie de Vivre Hotels (JDV Hospitality)**

JDV Hospitality is a successful boutique hotel company based in San Francisco. Chip Conley, its founder and CEO, believes strongly that brand and culture are synonymous. He has even written a book, entitled *The Rebel Rules: Daring to Be Yourself in Business*, in which he describes his business philosophy and rules for success. He asserts that most companies do not follow a recipe for culture, pursuing instead a half-hearted trial-and-error approach that rarely results in adding value to the development of the organization. JDV's social fabric is the result of following a recipe for culture. This is articulated through a key concept encapsulated in the phrase "In the first five minutes, inspire all five senses" and reinforced through several internal mechanisms designed to reinforce the social fabric of JDV.

"In the first five minutes, inspire all five senses" inspires JDV to work hard to stimulate the senses of anyone who visits one of its hotels. This applies to employees and passers-by as much as it does to overnight guests. But it is not a license for garish or over-the-top displays of false service, pounding music or overly cute furnishings. Each of JDV's 25 hotels offers the five-senses experience, each based on its unique personality. For example, the Hotel Rex is designed for people who love books and the feel of old bookstores or libraries. In the lobby, soft music is playing in the background while the faint scents of leather, books and rich woods permeate the air. The hotel looks like a classic library — warm, inviting and relaxing. Fresh fruit is on the front desk, available for guests to sample. The rich aromas wafting from the hotel's restaurant, Café Andree, gracefully awaken your appetite. The service is first rate: friendly, even charming, and thoughtful. The front-desk staff is solicitous, offering to arrange any manner of excursions as you check in to your room. They exude a genuine passion for San Francisco, books and food. All five senses are stimulated in the first five minutes. Multiply this effect by JDV's 24 other hotels and you can imagine how each one offers a delightful sensory experience. The management challenge is to create 25 unique guest experiences yet offer consistently excellent service. It is the antithesis of the cookie-cutter model so often used in hospitality, and it works very well for JDV.

How does JDV do this? By supporting and fostering an atmosphere that is collegial, service oriented and passionately devoted to JDV Hospitality's ideals. To do this well requires a strong effort in listening to employees. Chip Conley and his team conduct an annual internal "work-climate" survey. Employees answer questions anonymously about compensation, working conditions, what they like and don't like, and a host of company-related questions, all designed to garner feedback about the quality of the work experience. The results are analyzed by a third-party research firm and the findings are discussed by all employees at a series of off-site retreats. Chip and his executive team, along with the employees, have open discussions about JDV Hospitality, what makes the company great and what needs to be done to make it better.

Separately, a team of cultural ambassadors visits each of the hotels several times each year to review (effectively, a qualitative audit) whether each hotel is living the company's philosophy. These visits are not scheduled, so hotel staff don't know when they will happen. The resulting review is written and given to the hotel's management team for use in improving their operation.

Each hotel also conducts two front-office/back-office meetings each month to keep each area aware of the other's needs. These allow front-office staff to understand what back-office people are dealing with, which also influences behavior with guests, and they connect the back-office staff to the efforts of the front-office people, offering insight into what it is like working with the public. The meetings expose each of the groups to the sensitivities of the other, indirectly facilitating more effective support between them.

The work-climate survey, the cultural ambassadors, and the front-office/back-office meetings are directed internally and help the company understand whether it is on track with its message and execution.

Externally, the company surveys its guests through its standard in-room comment card, which it reviews each month. Even more interesting, however, is a "split-second" survey that JDV conducts each month at every hotel. Hotel staffers survey 30 guests at random during the month (whether at the lobby, in the hall, on their way to dinner or in the lounge). The goal is to get "the pulse of the guest experience" and not a scientific, statistically significant set of data results. JDV wants to understand what the guest experience is like and it takes the anecdotal comments seriously. Such surveys provide JDV Hospitality with useful feedback that further enables it to determine how successful it is in delivering its "five-senses" experience.

WHERE'S THE DATA?

The data for culture resides in several internal areas. HR contains firm-wide information on compensation levels. HR also probably has information on the amount spent, in total and per employee, on annual training. Furthermore, each department may also have its individual training budgets per employee that are separate and distinct from those of HR. Finance, or perhaps each department, may have specific figures on productivity per employee. As we saw from Joie de Vivre Hospitality, the data is found in a blend of internal and external surveys that combine qualitative and quantitative measures. To suggest a hard-and-fast rule would be foolhardy simply because each company is different and the measures used should be designed with a keen eye on the culture and personality of the company.

There are several general qualitative and quantitative measures that help ascertain performance levels.

The top performers in any organization are usually well known and, in any event, should be easily identified through their ongoing performance. Department bosses, colleagues, senior managers and HR representatives all know who are the rising stars in the organization. But to truly understand what makes them the best requires that you have a clear understanding of the criteria against which this can be judged. These may include such things as performance in the areas of sales, productivity and profitability. You might also consider the extent to which an employee exceeds set goals and quotas and how well they understand and support the company and its brand strategy. Important, too, are the behaviors they exhibit. (Are they open and honest? Are they enthusiastic in their work and are they willing to help others? Do they have the respect of their colleagues? and so on.)

CALCULATING IT

Measuring culture is a bit nebulous, given its highly qualitative tools and behavioral characteristics. But there are ways to ascertain employee performance resulting from the application of the various Magic Numbers in this section, mostly around productivity.

Calculating productivity per employee is straightforward. For example, productivity can measure the average revenues generated per employee. This is calculated by taking the total revenues and dividing them by the total number of employees, to arrive at a revenue figure per employee.

It can be determined by measuring costs in total and per employee, with the difference between revenues and costs per employee offering a sense of the profit each employee contributes.

Productivity can also be measured based on the conversion of customer targets to sales, effectively prescribing a yield (the percentage of converted prospects, with the higher the percentage indicating a higher yield and a more effective rate of sales closure).

What it Means and Potential Challenges

What brand-culture means to the value of the firm, however, goes beyond the tangible measures of productivity per employee. It involves attaching value to the invisible forces of culture, which are not easily distilled down to a few succinct formulas. As a case in point, apply the concept of culture to its more typical association: a country. When we think of a country — France, for example — we can describe its culture. Of course, asking any two people what the French culture is will likely yield different answers. Ask 200 people and some commonalities may emerge. Expand your survey to 20,000 people and additional common points are found. One can imagine the range of answers: French culture is "wine, cheese, bread, art, music, Napoleon, the Eiffel Tower, language…". The list is extensive, as it would be for any country. But the important point is that we can all articulate what French culture is (and is not) and while the answers would not likely be identical, they would all (or mostly) reflect French culture. But how do you measure it exactly? On the basis of its colorful history and contribution to art? How do you attach a specific value to it?

The same holds true for a company. Ask anybody to describe Singapore Airlines and its culture, and the answers will likely range from "the Singapore Girl" to "Exotic" to "Friendly…" . But what is the tangible, measurable value of these components of culture? They are hard to pin down. Yet without them, the airline would be valued less by passengers.

[1] The 4Ps are also called the "marketing mix". Each "P" is a variable that marketers can use to create value for customers: Product, Price, Place (distribution) and Promotion. They help marketers organize and describe their offerings to the market.

[2] The 5Cs provide a framework for marketing analysis. Each "C" is a component of a general market analysis: Company, Customer, Competition, Collaborators and Context. Marketers use the 5Cs to describe the factors that influence their final product/service decisions.

[3] Angel investors are private citizens who invest money into companies. They are typically high-net-worth individuals who are interested in helping start-up companies gain funding. They are not nearly as formal in structure as venture-capital firms. Angel investors usually, but not always, invest seed money that helps the start-up stay afloat while it continues to attract larger capital infusions from venture capitalists. Angel investors are a key part of the high-tech market in the U.S. and Europe and are only now emerging in Asia.

Part Three

MAGIC NUMBERS FOR UNDERSTANDING CUSTOMERS

MAGIC NUMBERS FOR UNDERSTANDING CUSTOMERS

Knowledge of customers is both a science and an art. This section will look more at the science of it: how to measure customer costs and life-time value, for example. The art side is a separate field unto itself and is intrinsic to the building of relationships with customers. Some of this was discussed in Magic Number 24, Brand Culture Framework.

Segment Profitability

THE DEFINITION

While marketers are, often deservedly, accused of focusing only on revenues, there are tools that enable them to measure revenue growth resulting from their marketing efforts, as well as the profitability of those efforts. Segment profitability allows marketers to measure whether an attractive segment from a revenue standpoint will also be profitable.

THE FORMULA AND ITS COMPONENTS

Three formulas are used to measure segment profitability.

1.

$$C_{nm} = \{D_s \times S_s \times (P_{pu} \times M)\} - E_m$$

Where

C_{nm} = net marketing contribution
D_s = segment demand
S_s = segment share
P_{pu} = price per unit
M = percentage margin
E_m = marketing expense

2.

$$\text{Marketing ROS} = \frac{C_{nm}}{S} \times 100\%$$

Where

S = sales

3.

$$\text{ROI} = \frac{C_{nm}}{E_m} \times 100\%*$$

This is the third variation for ROI referred to in Magic Number 35.

WHERE'S THE DATA?

Segment demand and segment share statistics are gathered through market research. Primary research would be conducted or commissioned directly by your company to study the market. However, your industry may have trade journals that publish annual statistics. Even general business magazines will often cite such statistics. The net marketing contribution, margin percentages, marketing expenses and price per unit are all found in your detailed account records for each customer, which are probably summarized in the income statement. The marketing plan and programs may also list pricing information, although this is likely to be in a more hypothetical "ideal world" stage and not in the actual market data.

CALCULATING IT

We will look at how to calculate profitability using a couple of hypothetical case studies.

Example 1: Kool Bicycles

Kool Bicycles is based in the Southeast Asia region. Demand for bicycles across Malaysia, Thailand, Viet Nam, Cambodia, Laos, Indonesia and Singapore is three million bicycles per year. Kool Bicycles has been in this market for 20 years and has developed a strong reputation for reliable and affordable bicycles targeted at the entry-level consumer. It has been able to garner a 25% market share in what is otherwise a fragmented industry. Kool's bikes are built of quality parts but have few extra features, thus selling for S$50. By contrast, premium bikes with composite materials, sophisticated gear technology and state-of-the-art shocks sell for as much as S$1,500. Bicycle manufacturing is expensive because of the number of parts that are put together by hand. Kool's main facilities are located in Sri Lanka, Cambodia and Laos, where wages are lower. Consequently, Kool's costs are slightly more manageable than most competitors in the industry, which helps

Kool maintain 15% margins. Because many of Kool's customers live in emerging economies, traditional marketing, such as print advertising and billboards, is both expensive and yields a low response. Consequently, it focuses its marketing efforts on point-of-purchase (POP) displays and minor promotional giveaways such as seat covers and reflectors. Its total marketing expenses are 10% of sales.

These figures are plugged directly into the formulas:

$$C_{nm} = \{D_s \times S_s \times (P_{pu} \times M)\} - E_m$$
$$= \{3,000,000 \times 25\% \times (50 \times 15\%)\} - \$3,750,000$$
$$= \$1,875,000$$

This means that Kool's efforts to target the entry-level bike buyer in Southeast Asia have a net marketing contribution of $1,875,000.

Now, let's bring in the other two formulas to fully measure the attractiveness of this segment:

$$ROS = \frac{C_{nm}}{S} \times 100\%$$

$$ROS = \frac{\$1,875,000}{\$37,500,000} \times 100\%$$

$$= 5\%$$

$$ROI = \frac{C_{nm}}{E_m} \times 100\%$$

$$ROI = \frac{\$1,875,000}{\$3,750,000} \times 100\%$$

$$= 50\%$$

As you can see, Kool's return on sales is 5% and its return on investment is 50%. These results may be very consistent with the bicycle industry overall, but Kool would have to compare its figures with other manufacturers to help determine if this is a good performance. Of course, Kool would have its own internal performance expectations as well; if these results are similar, then Kool ought to be pleased. Let's look at another example.

Example 2: Tea Baggers

Tea Baggers is a new company. It started only four years ago with the intention of producing and selling a wide variety of fruit-flavored herbal teas. The demand for tea in Singapore, Tea Baggers' primary market, is quite high, with over 20 million boxes sold annually (each box holds 12 bags of tea, and Tea Baggers has several box sizes. But the majority of its business is driven by the 12-bag box). As a relatively new company, Tea Baggers is still growing its market share in a business dominated by large multinational corporations (MNCs). Despite this competition, Tea Baggers has managed to achieve a 7% share in this market. The 12-bag box is priced at $10. Tea Baggers has a clever approach to purchasing ingredients for its tea: it acquires the rejected tea leaves from its competitors' suppliers at steep discounts, knowing that the addition of fruit flavorings reduces the otherwise acidic taste of the lower-quality leaves. Consequently, Tea Baggers' margins are a robust 35%. Because Tea Baggers is marketing products in a mature, highly competitive industry, it has to offer promotional allowances, slotting allowances, point-of-purchase displays and co-op advertising commitments to its network of retailers to secure consistent distribution and placement. Its marketing costs are therefore 30% of sales. Tea Baggers targets younger consumers who like variety and perceive the fruit-flavored teas as unique and different from the more traditional black teas that their parents prefer. Tea Baggers wants to review the segment profitability of this audience. Here is how its analysis looks:

$$C_{nm} = \{D_s \times S_s \times (P_{pu} \times M)\} - E_m$$
$$= \{20,000,000 \times 7\% \times (10 \times 35\%)\} - \$4,200,000$$
$$= \$700,000$$

$$ROS = \frac{C_{nm}}{S} \times 100\%$$

$$ROS = \frac{\$700,000}{\$10,000,000} \times 100\%$$
$$= 7\%$$

$$ROI = \frac{C_{nm}}{E_m} \times 100\%$$

$$\text{ROI} = \frac{\$700,000}{\$4,200,000} \times 100\%$$

$$= 16.7\%$$

Tea Baggers' efforts to reach the younger audience have resulted in a net marketing contribution of $500,000. Its return on sales is 7% and the return on investment is 16.7%. These figures may strike you as low, as well they may be. But in the competitive world of non-durable consumer products, this type of result is fairly predictable. Unless your volumes are quite large, an advantage the MNCs have because of their global distribution and supply-chain efficiencies, then smaller companies like Tea Baggers face significant challenges competing against the giants and earning stronger returns.

WHAT IT MEANS AND POTENTIAL CHALLENGES

Segment profitability is a useful method to assess both the attractiveness and success of specific audiences you are targeting. It can help companies understand how different components of their marketing investments affect profitability, which can guide marketing decisions for the future. Each segment, however, is likely to be unique and success (or failure) in one does not guarantee a similar performance in another. Marketers need to use the various marketing tools at their disposal to adjust the value proposition, ensuring that they are fine-tuning their efforts based on the characteristics of a given segment. This is one of the central challenges in marketing and it is a reason why marketers and their marketing efforts can often be disappointing in the eyes of CFOs and CEOs. Marketers will implement a campaign consistent across multiple segments, yet only one segment may respond favorably. Consequently, the overall marketing effort looks wrong; yet the useful lesson is the response of the segment that found the proposition attractive. Marketers must develop their budgets and programs with an eye toward the different programs required to reach each audience BEFORE going to market, so that the power of marketing can be fully realized.

This may strike many marketers as wrong. After all, isn't one of marketing's "rules" to develop a consistent image? Yet I am recommending different programs for different segments because marketers need to separate an overall consistent brand image from nuanced communication and specific appeals tailored to the mindset of each audience. The two go hand in hand. For example, BMW has long had a reputation for superior-quality luxury cars. In its marketing efforts, it has targeted multiple audiences: successful business people with the 7 Series, adventurous yuppies with the SUVs, and sports-car enthusiasts with the Z3 and Z4. BMW's overall image of quality and luxury remains constant, yet its message to different audiences is unique.

I hope the point is clear: segment profitability is an analytical approach that can help you better understand your success at appealing to each audience AND to recognize the importance of varying your marketing program in line with the unique characteristics of each audience.

Loyalty Frameworks

Loyalty is highly sought by most successful companies, yet not very well understood. Why is it important? It directly influences brand value and brand equity. The simplistic answer we hear is that it is less expensive to retain existing customers than to attract new ones. That has some truth, although loyal customers can also be more demanding, with higher expectations, conceivably costing you more to service their inflated expectations. On the other hand, a lack of loyalty means customers don't find your offerings worth a second look. That, too, is expensive. On balance, loyalty tends to enhance brand value and brand equity because it stabilizes financial performance (we know where our revenues are coming from and how much it costs to service our best customers) and builds relationships between the company and consumers, helping both understand each other better. Much like sports fans develop loyalties to their favorite teams and the teams, in turn, want to win to keep the fans coming back, companies that want to build brand value must work hard to keep their customers coming back.

THE DEFINITIONS

Customer Loyalty

This indicates not only how satisfied customers are with a company's products but, more importantly, how committed customers are to that brand, company or product. This commitment is often demonstrated when a customer recommends the product or service to others.

Brand Loyalty

From the customer's point of view, brand loyalty describes the general belief, commitment and trust that the customer has in the brand. This can also be described as company loyalty.

Retail Loyalty

This describes customers that are devoted to a retailer, or set of retailers, and arises from a number of factors, including convenience, selection, price, reputation and service.

Product Loyalty

Product loyalty refers to the customer's preference for that product category and/or specific product brands within. Product loyalty can be sub-divided into *same product/same company* and *same product/different company*.

Same product/same company refers to customers who buy the same product from the same company regularly. Classic examples include cigarettes, colas, and even coffee.

Cigarette customers are among the most loyal customers, rarely switching brands or products because they get used to very specific tastes (menthol, for example). Of course, one could argue that these customers are addicted and have little choice unless they want to go through unpleasant side-effects that include irritability, the "shakes", hacking and so forth.

Cola customers are also quite loyal. Coke does taste different from Pepsi. Personally, I prefer Coke, but my kids think I'm nuts and that Pepsi tastes better. Cola companies spend a fair amount of money and time on advertising in an effort to connect to us emotionally. This has proven mostly successful over the years, with Pepsi consistently associated with a more youthful audience (remember "The Choice of a New Generation" and "Come Alive with the Pepsi Generation"?) and Coke is associated with a slightly older and, arguably, more discerning audience (recall "Coke is It" and "It's the Real Thing").

Same product/different company refers to customers who are loyal to a product, say disposable razors, but not as concerned with a brand (usually because the products are perceived as commodities and, thus, are easily changed without any reduction in performance). For companies, this type of customer can be maddening, since loyalty is hardly assured despite significant expenditures in marketing programs, advertising and sales forces. However, these customers can also represent high value should you be clever enough to devise a truly differentiated product that disrupts the existing standards and attracts previously indifferent customers to your product. When this occurs, you have obviously converted a customer to same product/same company product loyalty.

Examples

Luxury-goods companies like LVMH (Louis Vuitton Moet Hennessey), BMW, Cunard (five-star luxury cruises on QEII and Queen Mary) and Rolex have very loyal customers. Their respective customers often support the overall brand, even if they are not regular purchasers of the same product within the brand. This is often the result of their affinity for the image and personality that the brand represents. It also reflects the emotional connection customers make with these brands, as they often see these companies as extensions of themselves.

LVMH

LVMH is the world's largest and most valuable luxury-products company. It has over 50 luxury brands under the LVMH umbrella in a diverse range of product categories, including perfumes and cosmetics, luggage, watches, champagnes and cognacs, and apparel. The LVMH brand includes handbags adorned with the ubiquitous and distinctive. LVMH logo, exclusive Tag Heuer watches and the best champagnes in the world. Undoubtedly, many LVMH customers buy products from several of its brands because they know that the LVMH brand represents prestige overall and, by extension, the products within are prestigious by association.

BMW

A BMW customer may own both a Z4 and a 7 Series car for love of BMW's brand (and its reputation for quality and engineering), yet appreciate the unique differences of each product (the Z4's sports-car look and feel as against the 7 Series' spaciousness and assorted luxury appointments).

Cunard

Cunard's loyal customers often travel on multiple cruises, on trips that vary from a few days to a couple weeks. Or, they may choose the Queen Mary due to its sheer size and impressiveness, while also enjoying the more personal cruises on the Caronia. All are different product adventures, but each is also a Cunard-branded product.

They do so because they can afford to, because they love the old-world charm represented by Cunard's 170-plus years of tradition and they love the pampered exclusivity that defines the service. Each of these contributes to customer loyalty. Cunard works hard to make this happen. It has a detailed database of its best customers and it spends the time getting to know them. Its customers know and appreciate this. Most of all, 170 years of five-star cruise experiences have made Cunard the recognized leader in this niche market. Generations of Cunard customers have passed down stories of cruising in world-class comfort to exotic locales with the most famous passengers one can imagine. These stories make quite a powerful impact and enhance the prestige and deepen the loyalty because passengers want to be part of this very special experience.

Rolex

Rolex offers several statement-watch collections. A Rolex customer may find that both an elegant Oyster watch and the classic Submariner are appealing for entirely different reasons, yet share the common image of superior quality. The Oyster Collection watches convey sophistication and opulence, while the Submariner's appeal lies in its rugged, durable design. In all cases, Rolex represents premium value and it builds relationships with its customers based on this. Customers develop loyalty because they see Rolex as special, which reflects their self-image. Rolex would risk this loyalty if it were to offer discounted watches, and this would diminish its brand value and unique market position.

Similar behaviors can be observed, too, in the gourmet coffee market and the hotel industry, as the following examples show.

Starbucks

Coffee customers are among the most recent consumers to have developed loyalty, particularly in the U.S., thanks partly to Starbucks and its massive growth the past decade. Starbucks customers are loyal both to the coffee and to the experience of being in the store itself. The experience dimension is interesting because it reveals that there can be far more to loyalty than merely a product. In fact, in Starbucks' case, the experience and the coffee are so closely intertwined that many customers see them as one in the same.[1] Interestingly, the large-scale loyalty Starbucks has developed has helped create a backlash that has facilitated loyalty *against* Starbucks and in favor of a local or competing brand.

Espresso Connection

Espresso Connection in Seattle, Washington, is another example of a company with high loyalty from customers preferring the same product from the same company. Founded by a high-energy entrepreneur named Christian Karr, Espresso Connection has developed into an 11-store chain. It has been around nearly as long as Starbucks, but its loyalty comes from customers who not only do not like Starbucks, but crave a different kind of coffee experience. Like Starbucks, Espresso Connection roasts its own beans and has developed its own signature flavors. Its "experience" is very different from Starbucks, yet uniquely appealing. Many of its coffee stores are located near busy intersections and high-traffic areas. That by itself is not unique. But what is unique is the store design. The outlets I visited have double drive-through windows rather than the more standard single drive-through. This effectively gives Espresso Connection twice as much opportunity to sell coffee to drive-by motorists. Furthermore, its service design is also unique. Coincidentally, each time I drove up to the window, I happened to be the third car in line. While the first car waited at the pick-up window and the second car was at the ordering box, an employee cheerfully skipped (yes, skipped) out of the store directly to my car to take my order. Each time, the employee smiled, asked me what kind of coffee I wanted and offered me a free sample of food. On the first occasion, the employee asked me if I wanted to hear the joke of the day. At the other store I was told of headline news events. Either way, it was entertaining and definitely not the typical coffee-buying experience. Since I do not live in Seattle I cannot be considered a loyal customer, but I am committed to telling these stories because they were such delightful examples of service designed to garner loyalty.

Marriott

Marriott's loyalty is derived from its reputation for consistency across its hundreds of locations. It is loyalty based on convenience and common expectations. Guests of Marriott know what to expect when visiting one of its hotels: reliable service, clean and basic rooms, reasonable rates. As Marriott grew, it developed new concepts to cover more segments of the market: long-term travelers (people who may stay in one location for a week or longer) stay at Marriott Residence Inns; business travelers who like the suites concepts stay at Courtyard by Marriott; families, who prefer the resorts, stay at Marriott Resorts and Spas (such as that in Bangkok, Thailand); and the upscale traveler, who prefers the Ritz Carlton hotels. Each of these Marriott sub-brands caters to a niche market, although a large enough niche in each hotel group to warrant hundreds of sister properties around the world.

Joie de Vivre Hospitality

As we saw in Magic Number 24, the Joie de Vivre hotel company earns a very different type of loyalty. The founder, Chip Conley, believes strongly that travelers seek unique experiences. His customers are loyal not because every hotel is the same, but because every hotel is different. Each property caters to a different niche, based partly on the target customer's personal interests. For example, the Hotel Rex is designed and devoted to books. The Hotel Phoenix, the company's first hotel, has developed a reputation as a "rock 'n' roll" hotel and it is even a favorite destination for bands and musicians that perform in San Francisco (including the Red Hot Chili Peppers, for example). The Hotel Del Sol is themed around art. You get the idea. Joie de Vivre's loyalty is not predicated on more typical product models, yet it works equally well.

Shangri-La Hotels

Shangri-La Hotels, based in Singapore, represents two hotel brands: Shangri-La and Traders. The Shangri-La brand is upscale, exclusive and premier. The properties are luxurious and the service is impeccable. Customers are loyal because they have come to expect the very best whenever staying at a Shangri-La property, of which there are now 44 around the Asia Pacific region. The Traders Hotels are a bit more relaxed and less sophisticated, although still very pleasant and well appointed. The service within the entire group is consistently excellent. I have visited the Traders Hotel in Yangon, Myanmar, several times and each visit is a testament to service excellence. The staff know me by name and they know the type of room I like. I see many of the same guests each time I visit, which is a telling, albeit anecdotal, example of their loyalty. I have also visited other Shangri-La properties in Singapore, Fiji, Thailand and Hong Kong and have always had the same high-quality experience.

Loyalty to Customers

The aforementioned definitions of loyalty described loyalty from customers to a company and/or its products. There is also loyalty from the company to its customers and entails the business nurturing customers during the pre-, during- and post-purchase phases. This view of loyalty reflects the company's commitment to attracting, developing and retaining its customer base. In this instance, a consumer-products firm is interested in maintaining strong relationships with its wholesale and retail customers to ensure continued product placement, promotion and general support. This is known in marketing as a *push* strategy, which refers to a consumer products company's efforts to persuade its channel[2] members to stock its products, which can have a strong influence on consumers. Consumer-products companies also want to appeal directly to consumers through advertising and promotions. This is known as a *pull* strategy, which describes the company's efforts to persuade consumers to request its products from the channel.

Pre-sales loyalty reflects the high interest level the sales rep has in learning about the retail customer, adapting product requirements or services to the specific needs of the customer in an effort to establish rapport, build confidence and set the stage for an eventual sale. In this phase, any contract terms are discussed and negotiated (volume pricing, payment terms…).

During-sales loyalty is the execution phase wherein the sales rep has already identified the buyer's needs, wants and requirements, adapted the offering accordingly, and received commitment from the buyer to purchase. In this phase, the contract is signed and the seller is committed legally to fulfilling the sale per the terms of the contract.

Post-sales loyalty describes the effort to support the customer following the completion of the sale. This can include warranty terms, support services and replacement guarantees.

THE FORMULA AND ITS COMPONENTS

Loyalty is not simply derived from a formula as it depends on the assumptions made. You must ask a series of questions to help determine the type of loyalty you are trying to understand. These include:

- Who is our typical customer?

- What is the profile of the ideal customer?

- How do we define "loyalty" (number of purchases, frequency of purchases, amount of purchases…)?

- What is profitable loyalty?

Once you have a clearer picture of your ideal customers, you can then start to determine whether your existing customers fit the profile.

WHERE'S THE DATA?

Customer-loyalty data can be found through a number of sources.

- Scanner data (with respect to grocery, pharmacy and supermarket customers)

- Loyalty cards and membership programs (retail, wholesale…)

- Reservations history (in the case of hotels, airlines, restaurants)

- Online-purchase patterns (via tracking software and customer-purchase history)

- Surveys and focus groups designed to ask purchase behavior

- Industry reports.

CALCULATING IT

As with the formula section above, calculating loyalty depends on the many variables and assumptions you use. Once you have outlined the characteristics that you think define a loyal customer, you can then evaluate data on your existing customers to determine how many fit your loyalty profile, how many are close, and how many are not loyal or are one-time/part-time purchasers.

WHAT IT MEANS AND POTENTIAL CHALLENGES

The key challenges to understanding loyalty are the assumptions you make and the variables you choose. You must recognize that no definition is perfect, but also realize that definitions based on convenience are not ideal either. Generally, loyalty is a mix of frequency of use or purchase over a sustained period of time, along with a reasonable level of profit. Obviously, you do not want loyal but unprofitable customers.

This was a challenge faced in the high-tech enterprise-software sector in the late 1990s. During that time, enterprise and web-enabled software solutions were extremely popular. This was driven partly by the rapid commercialization of the Internet, coupled with a wildly over-valued stock market and mind-boggling initial public offerings (IPOs) that seemed to suggest that all technologies were world class, all companies were outstanding, all entrepreneurs were geniuses and all people over 40 were doomed. Older database-software companies such as Oracle and Informix ("older" is a relative term as both of these companies were less than 20 years old, but were veritable dinosaurs amid the lightning-fast proliferation of "hot", new software firms) were in an unusual position. With the upstart tech firms gobbling up mind-share, dominating the media and giving away free products (software, for example), the older firms were forced to alter their pricing policies. Loyal customers of the database companies began seeking more aggressive terms from their suppliers, which often included selling the software at a discounted price and giving away the engineering support and customer service for up to a year. The result placed these firms in the unfortunate position of trying to keep long-term customers happy while losing more money on every sale because the cost to service complex enterprise-software products often exceeded the price of the software itself. Profitable loyalty had descended into unprofitable loyalty as vendors scrambled to satisfy increasingly demanding customers. It was a vicious circle that contributed to the eventual demise, or certainly severe shrinking, of numerous formerly formidable firms. The changes were so rapid that vendors had little time to educate or coach their customers about the dangers of the new-found demands for pricing reductions, partly because these firms were fearful of losing loyal, profitable and established customers to the newer competitors.

Loyalty, managed thoughtfully, can yield long-term, annuity-paying customer relationships that produce reasonable profits. [The word "annuity" in this context is applied to customers who return year after year.] On the other hand, there is the risk that loyal customers will expect more. The reason for this is that as customers get to know your company better and you them, they also expect a more personal and thoughtful level of service and product customization, which can lead to higher expense for you. Retail chains around the world are familiar with this pattern. Their most loyal customers shop in their stores for many reasons: selection, friendly people, location, prices, service. But over the years, as more discounters have entered the market, the older retailers have been forced to compete by offering the occasional sale. In the U.S., sales usually followed a major holiday, which over time led consumers to wait until after a holiday to purchase. This has even occurred during the Christmas season, although the tradition of Christmas still drives most of the pre-holiday sales. This has led to greater peaks and valleys in business cycles. As we saw earlier, the Robinsons department store in Singapore has found itself in the awkward position of being an almost-permanent place to window-shop until its annual sales begin.

Loyalty programs have had their strengths and weaknesses as well. For airlines, loyalty programs started out as a novel innovation to attract a more stable base of customers. Over many years they evolved into a ticking time-bomb of costs and lost revenues, as more and more frequent fliers accrued enough miles to fly many times each year for free. This has led major carriers to modify their programs to include more blackout periods (popular dates during which demand for air travel is highest) that are excluded from the frequent-flier mileage program awards.

Beyond the loyalty frameworks described above, extensive research has been conducted about loyalty and I encourage you to review the literature in greater detail. Sources such as *The Journal of Marketing Research*, *The Journal of Marketing*, the American Marketing Association (which has links to those journals at www.marketing-power.com) and the Marketing Science Institute offer remarkable insight into the factors that affect and influence loyalty. For example, while loyalty toward a brand does vary over time, there is little evidence to suggest that brand loyalty is eroding, despite claims to the contrary in the business press. As outlined in Magic Number 19, loyalty tends to remain high for market leaders,[3] and is far more complex than merely offering frequent-purchase programs or having great sales people. Additional research indicates that companies with enduring customer loyalty concentrate on several key variables: operations excellence (embedding loyalty practice into process), operations benevolence (how employees, particularly those on the front line, behave), problem-solving and management policies and practices. Each of these influences the development of trust between customers and companies.[4] Loyalty is also influenced by communications to the market, in message, design quality and medium.[5] While none of this may surprise you, examining the research in depth will illuminate the factors that influence loyalty and provide you with best practices you can incorporate into your company.

[1] Kochra, Ariff; Crosnan, Mary: "Starbucks", Case # 9A98M006 ©1997.

[2] "Channel" is another description of Place (or distribution) from the 4Ps.

[3] Dekimpe, Marnik G.; Mellens, Martin; Steenkamp, Jan Benedict; Abeele, Piet Vanden: "Erosion and Variability in Brand Loyalty", Marketing Science Institute Report #96-114 ©1996.

[4] Sirdeshmukh, Deepak; Singh, Jagdip; Sabol, Barry: "Consumer Trust, Value, and Loyalty in Relational Exchanges", Marketing Science Institute Report #01-116 ©2001.

[5] Leenheer, Jorna; Bijmolt, Tammo H.A.: "Adoption and Effectiveness of Loyalty Programs: The Retailer's Perspective", Marketing Science Institute Report #03-124 ©2003.

MAGIC NUMBER 27

New-Product Purchase Rate

While some of the Magic Numbers for Consumer Marketing have been around for quite some time, they still have relevance today. The new-product purchase-rate formula is one such example.[1] It is in a category of marketing models called "diffusion" (or, sometimes, "penetration") which attempt to provide guidance about the likely acceptance of a new product in a given market. Such models include:

- The Bass Model of Diffusion

- Everett Rogers' "Diffusion of Innovations" model

- The ACCORD model (Advantage-Complexity-Compatibility-Observability-Riskiness-Divisibility)

- Geoffrey Moore's "Technology Adoption Life Cycle" model.

THE DEFINITION

The new-product purchase-rate formula helps companies determine the penetration rate for new, non-durable consumer products. In effect, it provides guidance on the rate of acceptance of a new product over time, which can help determine the effectiveness of a company's marketing programs in building share and generating sales.

THE FORMULA AND ITS COMPONENTS

$$q_t = rq \, (1 - r)^{t-1}$$

Where

q_t = the % of total households (U.S. in this model) expected to try the product in period t

r = rate of penetration of untapped potential

q = the % of total households (U.S.) expected to eventually try the new product

t = period of time

Where's the Data?

The data on households is government census data, which is collected at different times in different countries. A quick search on the web provides numerous references to household data from Canada, the U.S., Australia, the U.K., Japan, and Europe (including parts of the former Eastern bloc). China's data is less reliable due to differences in collection techniques and some uncertainty over census dates and comprehensiveness. Parts of South America also have basic household census data online.

Calculating It

From here, we can make assumptions to demonstrate the formula. In this instance, I will insert hypothetical numbers for San Francisco:

r = 40% of the remaining potential new buyers are penetrated

q = 20% of San Francisco households will actually buy the product

t = period of time.

Let's input these figures into the formula over successive time periods to demonstrate the changes in penetration rates.

$$q_1 = rq\,(1 - r)^{1-1} = (0.4)(0.2)(0.6^0) = 0.080$$
$$q_2 = rq\,(1 - r)^{2-1} = (0.4)(0.2)(0.6^1) = 0.048$$
$$q_3 = rq\,(1 - r)^{3-1} = (0.4)(0.2)(0.6^2) = 0.028$$
$$q_4 = rq\,(1 - r)^{4-1} = (0.4)(0.2)(0.6^3) = 0.017$$
$$q_5 = rq\,(1 - r)^{5-1} = (0.4)(0.2)(0.6^4) = 0.010$$

This demonstrates that, over time, the rate of penetration decreases as that 20% of the potential population is attracted.

From here, you can determine sales by simply taking the resulting penetration rate for each period and multiplying it by the total number of San Francisco households, then multiplying by the expected price for the first purchase (each period is essentially "first purchase" expenditures) per household. At the time of writing, there are approximately 330,000 households in San Francisco. Furthermore, I will assume the first-time purchase price for this product is $50.

$$q_t = rq\ (1 - r)^{1-1} = 0.080 \rightarrow .08\ \times 330,000 \times \$50 = \$1,320,000$$
$$q_t = rq\ (1 - r)^{2-1} = 0.048 \rightarrow .048 \times 330,000 \times \$50 = \$792,000$$
$$q_t = rq\ (1 - r)^{3-1} = 0.028 \rightarrow .028 \times 330,000 \times \$50 = \$462,000$$
$$q_t = rq\ (1 - r)^{4-1} = 0.017 \rightarrow .017 \times 330,000 \times \$50 = \$280,500$$
$$q_t = rq\ (1 - r)^{5-1} = 0.010 \rightarrow .010 \times 330,000 \times \$50 = \$165,000$$

WHAT IT MEANS AND POTENTIAL CHALLENGES

For a marketer launching a new non-durable product, this is an interesting way to gauge its potential economic lifespan, assuming of course that there are no changes in target-customer penetration, audience size, product features or pricing. These latter caveats are the challenges. Furthermore, determining the potential market for your product out of the total household population and the rate of penetration is somewhat arbitrary. You can mitigate some of this guesswork by gathering industry and competitor statistics for similar products and infer the potential for your own. But it is still guesswork. Nevertheless, this is an interesting guide for a new-product launch.

Of course, as with many of the Magic Numbers, questions arise. How does one determine "r", the rate of penetration of untapped potential? This is a good question and the answer depends on several factors:

- the market you are in

- the ease of determining, reaching and converting customers in your market

- an estimate of the remaining potential customers to be converted.

Determining the number of potential customers in your market requires you to *learn* about your actual target market, which means that you will have to do more research. For example, let's assume that you are marketing a new product called the Disposable Talking Toaster and deduce, for a variety of reasons, that a strong market for this product is San Francisco, California. Of course, since the model looks at the number of households, you do some more research to learn that there are approximately 330,000 households in San Francisco. Since this Disposable Talking Toaster is a new product, there is no history to determine actual market penetration rates. But since you have launched products in San Francisco before, you have a sense of how many of the 330,000 households will actually buy a new product, which will tell you how much potential market is left. From there, your previous product launch experience might have told you that the penetration rate into the remaining untapped potential in a market is 45%. But because this is a new product, you are a bit more cautious and decide to err on the side of lower penetration, so you adjust it to 40%.

If you had had no previous experience in this market, however, you might look at how other companies have fared when launching products of a reasonably similar nature into the market.

In parts of Asia, such information may not be available, in which case you might want to consider the Bass Diffusion Model, which helps explain the rate of product adoption based on word-of-mouth and use by opinion leaders (media and other external coverage) to influence adoption. The Bass Diffusion Model is particularly appropriate for Asia given the word-of-mouth culture in much of the region. More information on this can be found at the Marketing Science Institute website, www.msi.org; and at the Value Based Management.nec website (www.valuebasedmanagement.net). The astute marketer will realize that this model, too, requires more in-depth understanding of markets, so more research should be conducted.

Suffice to say that predicting product adoption rates is a combination of science and art. The science comprises the data-collection techniques and subsequent analysis. The art is in deciding how much of the result should be believed, given the vagaries of consumer behavior. In other words, just because consumers say they are likely to buy your product does not mean they will behave in that way at the actual time of purchase. Intent does not necessarily lead to action or purchase, in other words. Once you realize this, then you are far more likely to understand and appreciate that these formulas are merely guides, and to test their accuracy, you have to actually go to market. Scary, isn't it? But then, if these models were literally 100% perfect in prediction, we'd all be a lot richer!

[1] The formula has its origin in an article by Louis A. Fourt and Joseph N. Woodlock, entitled "Early Prediction of Market Success for New Grocery Products", in the *Journal of Marketing*, October 1960, pp.31–38. More recent, in-depth, research has been conducted by Peter S. Faber, Bruce G.S. Hardie and Chun Yao Huang in their article "A Dynamic Changepoint Model for New Product Sales Forecasting", *Marketing Science*, Vol. 23, No. 1, Winter 2004, pp.50–65.

MAGIC NUMBER 28

Share of Customer

THE DEFINITION

This concept is similar to market share, except that share of customer describes your sales to a customer as a percentage of the customer's total purchases for products of your type (whereas market share, you may recall, equals your sales as a percentage of total sales of all companies in your product market). Another way to describe it is as "share of the customer's wallet".

THE FORMULA AND ITS COMPONENTS

This should look familiar, since it is the same formula as market share but with an explanatory note.

$$S_c = \frac{S}{M_{cs}}$$

Where

S_c = share of customer
S = your sales to that customer
M_{cs} = total of all customer spending on your product category

WHERE'S THE DATA?

Once again, the data is available in several areas. Your company's financial statements will describe your sales. Industry data from market-research firms, industry surveys, competitive intelligence from consultancies and even Wall Street industry reports are likely to have the information required to assess market share. Of course, part of the analysis does depend on your definition of your customer, as it does in virtually any other Magic Number. The real magic to making this number work for you is in having a thorough knowledge and understanding of your customers. Very few formulas can replace genuine interaction between people at different companies in which trust is built, information is shared and solutions are created that are mutually beneficial. (See the Five Ambassadors behavior measures in Magic Number 24. Practicing these and instilling them into your organizational practices will enable you to confidently determine your share of customer.)

CALCULATING IT

While market share will tell you that you have 60% share if you have six customers out of 10, share of customer analyzes it at the individual customer level, measuring the percentage share you have of the total dollars that that customer has available to spend. It essentially tells you how successful you are in getting a customer to devote more of his or her total spending on your products vis-à-vis those of your competitors.

For example, if one of your customers has $1 million to spend on products of your type, and you have made sales of $100,000 to that customer, then you have a 10% share of customer. Thus, a 60% overall market share may sound impressive, but at the individual customer level, you may find that you have a lower actual dollar commitment from individual customers. Conversely, of course, if you have sales of $900,000 to that customer, then your share of customer is 90%.

WHAT IT MEANS AND POTENTIAL CHALLENGES

Share of customer is an interesting variation of market share, since it deals with the potential dollars customers have available to spend on your products as opposed to the sheer number of customers in the total market for your types of products. Whether you choose market share, market penetration or share of customer as a key measure, or all three, it is more important to ensure you understand what it is you are measuring.

MAG1C NUM8ER

29

Customer Investment

THE DEFINITION

This is the maximum marketing investment needed to create a given level of profitability per customer.

THE FORMULA AND ITS COMPONENTS

$$I_c = \frac{M_g}{(1 + ROI)}$$

Where

I_c = customer investment
M_g = gross margin
ROI = return on investment

As you can already see, to determine the level of customer investment that results in a maximum profit per customer requires a necessary first step: calculating ROI, as described in Magic Number 35. There you will find two definitions of marketing ROI — Classic ROI and Cost-based ROI. Since Cost-based ROI is demonstrated in that section, I will illustrate Classic ROI below. First, here is the formula for Classic ROI:

$$ROI = \frac{P_n}{A_t}$$

Where

P_n = net profit
A_t = total assets (or total investment)

WHERE'S THE DATA?

The data inputs are determined internally by senior management and the company's strategic plan, assuming you have one. If you do not, then I encourage you to outline and seek agreement on key marketing objectives, such as target markets, positioning, customer segments and marketing program budgets. Are these easy to create? Most likely not. But without this information you will find it exceedingly challenging to determine how much you should spend to achieve a certain level of customer profitability, essentially relegating your marketing efforts to sheer guesswork. While I advocate creativity and flexibility in developing marketing, I do not encourage career suicide, so you should spend time and effort determining these fundamental marketing components. Net profit information should be available from your finance or accounting departments. If they are interested in developing successful revenue streams from products and services, then it is likely they will want to help you.

CALCULATING IT

ROI calculations are expressed as a percentage rather than a financial amount. However, determining an appropriate ROI for your situation is entirely up to you. Your company may have very aggressive financial targets that require large, rapid returns to justify investment. On the other hand, a more patient, measured approach may be compatible with your company's behavior, with a moderate return expected. Any ROI below these set rates results in the project (or customer acquisition, in this case) not being funded. If you have never considered ROI before, then this is as good a starting time as any. Knowing how to determine a "reasonable" ROI is industry-specific and may even be company-specific, so before embarking on this analysis, I recommend you do a bit of homework to learn about similar investments in your industry. This will give you some sense of typical ROIs for similar investments from others in your market space. For the sake of simplicity, I will use the following hypothetical example.

GameBrainer is a leader in the electronic video-game market, making thrilling action games about home-cooking disasters, targeted toward teens and, of course, future restaurateurs. GameBrainer has decided to launch a new game that allows users to experience the non-stop excitement of Samurai combat while simultaneously making sushi. It decides that it is only worth launching this product if it can get an ROI of 30%. Anything below that and the project is cancelled.

GameBrainer considers budgeting $2 million in advertising, hoping to generate a $3 million gross profit. To determine net profit, you must subtract the investment amount from the expected gross profit. A quick calculation reveals that this results in an ROI of 50%, as follows:

$$\text{ROI} = \frac{\$3,000,000 - \$2,000,000}{\$2,000,000}$$

$$= 50\%$$

The 50% ROI exceeds the company's 30% target, so it agrees to go forward with the Cooking Disaster game project. Knowing the ROI figure helps GameBrainer evaluate its maximum customer investment using the formula:

$$I_c = \frac{P_g}{(1 + \text{ROI})}$$

Let's further assume that the gross profit (P_g) from acquiring each customer is targeted at $500. Now we can calculate the customer investment required, as follows:

$$\text{CI} = \frac{\$500}{(1 + 30\%)}$$

$$= \$384$$

Thus, GameBrainer can invest $384 per customer to achieve the $500 gross profit. This satisfies the company's ROI requirement of 30% ($116/$384 = 30.2%).

The GameBrainer managers are ecstatic, of course. But the CFO then asks, "How many customers do you expect to actually convert from those that you reach?" This forces the marketers to conduct further research, from which they learn that customer conversion rates in the game industry are 15%. So they have to scale down their per-customer investment accordingly:

$$\$384 \times 15\% = \$57.60$$

When you have reached this point in your own calculations, it would be sensible to spend some time extending the analysis so that you can understand your various customer-investment thresholds, as follows:

Customer-investment levels (30% ROI threshold)

Gross $ Profit	Customer Conversion Rate (rounded)					
	1%	5%	15%	30%	100%	
$200	$1	$8	$23	$46	$154	
$300	$2	$12	$35	$70	$231	
$400	$3	$15	$46	$92	$308	Spending
$500	$4	$19	$58	$116	**$384**	per
$600	$5	$23	$69	$138	$462	customer
$700	$6	$27	$81	$162	$538	
$800	$7	$31	$92	$184	$615	

The benefit to this extended analysis is that it enables you to visualize how much you can spend per customer to achieve a certain gross profit, based on the 30% ROI target in this case.

WHAT IT MEANS AND POTENTIAL CHALLENGES

Customer investment is a helpful tool to evaluate the right level of spending per customer to achieve a specified return. A caution is needed here, however. ROI analysis, which is obviously factored into this analysis, is not always the most reliable measure because the denominator, total assets, is taken from the company's balance sheet and, depending on the age, the asset values may no longer reflect replacement costs. Therefore, undervalued assets can inflate the ROI. Should you choose the asset value to be equivalent to the amount invested, as we did in this analysis, then you again risk understating or misrepresenting the true values if you do not have clear, updated figures.

MAGIC NUM8ER

30 Customer-Acquisition Costs

THE DEFINITION

Customer-acquisition costs are those associated with acquiring a new customer.

THE FORMULA AND ITS COMPONENTS

Customer-acquisition cost is calculated by dividing total acquisition expenses by total new customers.

However, there are different opinions as to what constitutes an acquisition expense. For example, rebates and special discounts do not represent an actual cash outlay, yet they have an impact on cash (and, presumably, on the customer). To simplify this process, let's assume your company wants to calculate the cost of acquiring customers through one of its marketing vehicles, CD mailers. AOL used to do this regularly. Parts suppliers and several music distributors use this marketing approach as well, among others.

The formula for customer-acquisition costs in both examples is:

$$C_{ac} = CD_m \times C$$

Where

C_{ac} = customer-acquisition costs
CD_m = number of CD mailers needed to acquire one customer
C = cost to send each mailer

OR

$$C_{ac} = \frac{C}{R_r}$$

Where

R_r = response rate

WHERE'S THE DATA?

Fortunately, now that we're in the 21st century, there is a sizable body of data from multiple companies and product categories that offers excellent benchmarks for ascertaining direct-marketing metrics. Much of the data depends on who your target audience is. Once you determine who you would like to reach, you can do your own random mailing or you can find a list broker who has names for that particular audience. The list broker is usually a more cost-effective approach, as the ensuing examples will demonstrate.

Also, the costs for the marketing vehicle (in this example, CD mailers, but the same approach can be used with other media) depend on the numbers of CDs you send with each mailing and whether you include additional literature. Response rates are based on industry trends and, therefore, should not be guessed. If you do not know the response rates for your particular products, then try to find a reasonably similar industry and benchmark your metrics from those. In the worst case, if there are no comparable metrics, then assume a conservative response rate that is marginally better for rented lists than a purely random mailing (i.e. 2% response versus 1% response).

A question that inevitably arises is how to determine the number of CD mailers needed to acquire one customer ("CD_m"). This information will vary from one industry to the next and from one country to another. However, the Direct Marketing Association (DMA) website, www.the-dma.org, is a great place to obtain information. Within the site are links to other DMA sites in many countries around the world, including Singapore, Japan, Thailand, Australia and much of Europe, as well as North and South America. Contacting the relevant experts in each location and asking them how and where to find these metrics will help you determine a variety of metrics common to that country. It is important to do some homework for the country in which you are interested because often the general metrics cited are U.S.- or Euro-centric and may mislead you to think the same metric applies to your country or region. But the cultural differences around the world are vast and what is common practice in the U.S. may be quite different from what is common and acceptable in, say, Thailand.

However, once you have done your homework, you can then begin using this formula to benefit your analysis of your direct-marketing program (CD mailers, in this case). The "magic", then, in this number, is not in the general formula, but in using data and metrics that are consistent with the country context in which you are operating.

CALCULATING IT

Random mailing

Let's assume that the cost of mailing your CD mailers is $0.35 each, and the average response rate is 1% (perhaps based on your past experience sending mailers, or industry metrics…). Thus, one person will respond for every 100 CD mailers you send. The cost of acquiring each customer using a random mailing is:

First formula: $100 \times .35 = \$35$

Second formula: $\dfrac{\$0.35}{.01} = \$35$

Depending on the metrics for your industry as well as the average order size per customer, $35 to acquire a customer may be perfectly reasonable, too low or too high.

Acquired-list mailing

A smart marketer will not stop there, however. He or she will want to analyze other options to see if there are more effective ways to acquire customers. This marketer may know, or determine, that renting or acquiring a list of qualified prospects will yield a probable response rate of 3% (three times more effective than a random mailing). This means that for every 100 CD mailers sent, three people will respond. Thus, our marketer may decide to rent a list from a reputable list broker, knowing that the names on the list have a higher likelihood of purchasing the company's products. List brokers are in their business to make money and they expend a fair amount of effort to develop their lists through research, so they generally charge a fee. In this example, we'll assume the broker charges $0.25 per name.

The smart marketer can now compare the random mailing to the list mailing and decide which is better.

The cost of acquiring a customer using a list mailing is:

$$\frac{\$0.60}{.03} = \$20$$

The $0.60 is the simple result of the cost of mailing each CD, $0.35, plus the cost of acquiring each name, $0.25, divided by the response rate expected. The upfront cost of sending out CD mailers is clearly more expensive when a list is rented — 71% more in this example. But the overall cost of acquiring customers is reduced substantially AND the company is reaching an audience more likely to respond favorably to the company's offer.

WHAT IT MEANS AND POTENTIAL CHALLENGES

Acquisition costs vary across industries and media. When acquisition data is available, try to determine if you are comparing apples to apples. As discussed in the section above, using the formula success-fully means knowing more about the characteristics of the country market you are researching. For example, your research may reveal that your interest in sending CD mailers to prospective customers in the U.S. to promote your new line of "automatic nose hair braiders" will yield one new customer for every 25 mailers. "Great!" you shout, as you envision a day in the not-too-distant future when you are on the cover of *Fortune Magazine*, smiling, with a noticeably interesting facial feature. The image of increasingly vast riches float through your mind. You imagine the journalist who wrote your story asking where you will go next, to which you confidently reply, "Japan!" Then, when expanding to Japan, you discover from your research that you will need to send 100 CD mailers to acquire one customer. You then have to ask a few simple questions:

- Is sending 100 mailers reasonable, given the four-fold increase in costs?

- What is my break-even point when I cross that happy line from loss to profit?

- Is the longer-term market potential large enough to warrant the increased costs?

- Do I want to go to Japan?

Once you have run through the analysis, the final choice is yours. This is not always easy, as customer-acquisition data can be scarce, and the methodology is often foggy. Furthermore, it is a wise move to compare various list brokers and ask them for their customer names. Then, contact a few of their customers to learn whether the broker is as good as he or she claims. While list brokers will generally charge similar rates, there may be variation in quantity and quality of associated information with each name (i.e. some lists may come only with name and address, while others may come with name, address, company name, title and so on…). Brokers may also charge you more for each additional line of information you request beyond the basic name and address. Finally, list rentals are just that — rentals. You do not own the names in most cases. You only "own" the name once that target customer responds to your mailing. List brokers usually include several "dummy" contacts in their mailings to ensure you do not use their list more than once.

Customer Break-Even Analysis

THE DEFINITION

The core definition is that break-even is essentially the unit sales quantity required for a company's total costs to equal its total revenue. There are two approaches to break-even that I will describe in this section. It is important to see the different ways break-even is used since it affects other measures, such as lifetime customer-value analysis, and it is affected by other measures, such as customer-acquisition costs.

Knowing the cost of acquiring customers is helpful in determining when a customer will bring profits to the company. There are different types of customers, as we have discussed before. Developing long-term customer loyalty is usually the ideal, but only when loyalty leads to ongoing profitability. At some point, companies may have to face the decision of whether to keep a money-losing customer or setting them loose. The decision rests on your view of that customer's long-term potential and how long you are willing to stick with that customer until they are profitable.

Approach 1

Assuming that profitability is the goal, then it can also be assumed that there are customers who are frequent or regular purchasers of products, and customers who are infrequent or occasional purchasers of products. Let's look at both.

THE FORMULA AND ITS COMPONENTS

Break-even analysis is more than merely a formula, it is a series of data points based on the following components:

- Margin on each purchase

- Survival rate

- Cost of each marketing communication

- Expected profit per customer.

WHERE'S THE DATA?

Historical data will provide most of the information you need to understand each of your customers. Smart consumer-products companies know their customer purchase patterns if they sell direct (such as Dell) or if they sell through retailers (such as Nike). If you are a start-up company, don't lose hope. The lack of your own operating data shouldn't prevent you from determining customer break-even. Instead, you are dealing with a more hypothetical situation since you really don't know the behavior or patterns of your customers yet. But you can acquire industry data from benchmark companies and apply it to your target audience to get a sense of how long it will be before your customers, and ultimately your business, are profitable.

CALCULATING IT

Let's assume that Ravi's Amazing Auto Parts Company launches new products to the market twice per year, in winter and summer. Furthermore, we'll assume that Ravi's sends six CD mailers per year in the first year to all customer types. In the second year and beyond, regular customers will continue to receive six CD mailers each year. Less-frequent buyers, though, will receive only two per year thereafter as there is no need for Ravi to spend the money on them until they start buying more.

Since Ravi launches new products twice each year, his regular customers receive CD mailers with the same content for three consecutive mailings before he changes the CD mailer. Less-frequent customers obviously receive two different CD mailers with no repetition. The regular customers purchase Ravi's products three times each year, with an average order size of $30, while the less-frequent buyers purchase once each year, with an average order size of $60. The retention rate (the rate at which a customer is likely to return the following year) for regular customers is 90%, while the retention rate for less-frequent customers is 45%. Knowing the retention rates helps you determine the longer-term loyalty or survival rate of each group of customers (i.e. whether or not they will be around in a few years... you select the time period). In the case of the regular customer with a 90% retention rate, his loyalty or survival factor in year five is 65.6%.[1] The less-frequent customer's loyalty or survival rate in year five is 4.1%.[2]

It is also important to know the gross margin on each purchase, for obvious reasons: it helps you understand how many purchases a customer type must make over a given period of time before they become profitable. This will enable you to forecast how long you will be "investing" in CD mailers before converting that customer to profitability. Ravi's wants to know when its customers will be profitable using CD mailer marketing to acquire them. In this analysis, we will look at both sets of customers, using both the random-mailing approach and the rented-list approach to see the various break-even levels. The gross margin for Ravi's products is 25% of total sales. With these figures, we can construct comparisons between the regular and less-frequent customers with random and purchased list mailings.

Random Mailing

Review the assumptions:

Regular Customer

- Receives six CD mailers per year

- Makes three purchases per year, at $30 per purchase

- There is a 90% retention rate of regular customers who make purchases in the next time period

- Mailing cost = $0.35 per CD mailer

- 1% response rate

- Gross margin = 25%

Regular Customers	Year One	Year Two
Margin	$7.50	$7.50
Retention Rate	100%	90%
CD Mailing Cost	$.35 × 6 = $2.10	$.35 × 6 = $2.10
Profit per Customer	3 × 7.50 − 2.10 = $20.40	.9 × (22.50 − 2.10) = $18.36
Total Profits per Customer (factoring in acquisition costs)	$(14.60)	$3.76

Acquired Mailing

Review the assumptions:

Regular Customer

- Receives six CD mailers per year

- Makes three purchases per year, at $30 per purchase

- There is a 90% retention rate of regular customers who make purchases in the next time period

- Mailing cost = $.60 per CD mailer

- 3% response rate

- Gross margin = 25%

Regular Customers	Year One	Year Two
Margin	$7.50	$7.50
Retention Rate	100%	90%
CD Mailing Cost	$.60 × 6 = $3.60	$.60 × 6 = $3.60
Profit per Customer	3 × 7.50 − 3.60 = $18.90	.9 × (22.50 − 3.60) = $17.01
Total Profits per Customer (factoring in acquisition costs)	$(1.10)	$15.91

In this first set of examples with regular customers, you can see that acquiring a mailing list enhances profitability over the random mailing. Again, while the cost per mailing is higher by 71%, the customer-acquisition cost is lower with the acquired list, making the profit margin far higher. In this example, upfront investment in smart marketing (i.e. a mailing list) leads to larger profits. Costs, therefore, are not the only factor that should be considered when choosing a marketing program.

Now let's look at the same framework, but using less-frequent customers.

Random Mailing

Review the assumptions:

Less-frequent Customer

- Receives six CD mailers per year in year one, and two per year thereafter

- Makes one purchase per year, at $60 per purchase

- There is a 45% retention rate of regular customers who make purchases in the next time period

- Mailing cost = $.35 per CD mailer

- 1% response rate

- Gross margin = 25%

Less-Frequent Customers	Year One	Year Two	Year Three
Margin	$15	$15	$15
Retention Rate	100%	45%	20.25%
CD Mailing Cost	$.35 × 6 = $2.10	$.35 × 2 = $.70	$.35 × 2 = $.70
Profit per Customer	$15 − $2.10 = $12.90	.45 × (15 − .70) = $6.44	.2025 × (15 −.70) = $2.90
Total Profits per Customer (factoring in acquisition costs)	$(22.10)	($15.66)	($12.76)

As you can see, it will take several years using this approach before a less-frequent customer becomes profitable. The final example incorporates the cost of an acquired mailing list.

Acquired-list Mailing

Less-frequent Customer

- Receives six CD mailers per year in year one, and two per year thereafter

- Makes one purchase per year, at $60 per purchase

- There is a 45% retention rate of regular customers who make purchases in the next time period

- Mailing cost = $.60 per CD mailer

- 3% response rate

- Gross margin = 25%

Less-Frequent Customers	Year One	Year Two	Year Three
Margin	$15	$15	$15
Retention Rate	100%	45%	20.25%
CD Mailing Cost	$.60 × 6 = $3.60	$.60 × 2 = $1.20	$.60 × 2 = $1.20
Profit per Customer	$15 − $3.60 = $11.40	.45 × (15 − 1.20) = $6.21	.2025 × (15 − 1.20) = $2.79
Total Profits per Customer (factoring in acquisition costs)	$(8.60)	($2.39)	$40

WHAT IT MEANS AND POTENTIAL CHALLENGES

Customer break-even analysis appears relatively straightforward, but there are several less-visible factors that you must consider when undertaking it. As is evident from our simple examples, break-even is dependent on list quality, customer-retention rates, gross margin, mailing costs, purchase price and purchase frequency. This analysis ignored other variables such as when a company decides to stop sending its mailers to customers who are no longer active. Determining when a customer is no longer a customer should become part of your marketing program policies and planning, acknowledging that there will be exceptions. Assuming you plan annually, then it is reasonable to consider one year as the normal business cycle. Therefore, this decision would occur after the normal sequence of CD mailers has been sent since it will not be known until the end of a full year that a customer is no longer active. In this instance, you should modify your profit-per-customer calculations by multiplying the previous year's retention rate by the CD mailer's mailing cost. The reason for this is that the previous year is when the customer was last "active" and an influence on your profitability. You may also have other costs not reflected in this particular analysis, such as additional marketing promotions and communications connected to the CD mailer. These would have to be factored into your mailing cost if you have them. You may also have to review and adjust the final analysis of the CD mailer programs once you learn how many products are returned, cancelled or discounted. These challenges notwithstanding, customer break-even analysis is a very useful tool in assessing the potential of almost any marketing campaign. I use the word "almost" because this analysis is less reliable if you are attempting to correlate a general-awareness advertising campaign with increases in customers and sales. Unless the advertising campaign has a specific offer that asks for customers to respond, it is problematic linking an advertising campaign to any specific increase in business. This drives CFOs and many CEOs nuts (and many marketers, too), but it is a fact. Measurement enthusiasts will simply have to get comfortable with the idea that not everything is perfectly measurable.

Approach 2

The definition and formulas are effectively the same, so I will show you a different approach to calculating it. The key difference in this approach is that there are several different break-even formulas illustrated, each describing a different aspect of break-even. Together, they provide a robust set of measures that will enable you to evaluate the effectiveness of your product efforts.

CALCULATING IT

First, it is important to know how to calculate *contribution per unit* for the product you are selling. The contribution per unit is the amount of money that remains to cover fixed costs after all variable costs are deducted.

In this example, I will use the example of the Squeezer wallet first introduced in Magic Number 10. You may recall from that example that Ming is the product line manager and her main product, the Squeezer, retails for $10. Let's further assume that the retail margin is 30%. Since wholesalers are a key component of the value chain, they take an 8% margin. As mentioned previously, you have to know both fixed and variable costs to determine contribution per unit. The variable costs for the Squeezer are $3 per wallet. The total fixed costs (aggregate costs, not per unit) are $1,800,000 (salaries, equipment...).

As the new manager, Ming has come into a challenging situation. Despite this early success, the Squeezer is now facing reduced demand as a result of competition. Furthermore, customers are saying the Squeezer is overpriced. Ming is considering reducing the price by $2. But also due to her newness to this position and the challenges facing her product line, she is exploring hiring the pre-eminent consulting firm, McKinsey, to offer its consulting expertise since she does not want to jeopardize the Squeezer's early success with a hasty plan. Unfortunately, McKinsey is not cheap and has proposed a contract for $250,000 to help Ming for a month.

To complete her analysis and ensure her presentation to the board is ironclad, Ming works her way through several formulas to arrive at a break-even figure that is reasonable.

Let's review what we know so far about the Squeezer:

- Retails for $10
- Retail margins are 30%

- Wholesale margins are 8%

- Total market (TM) is 35 million customers

- Market share is 20%

- Variable costs are $3 per wallet

- Total fixed costs are $1,800,000

- Considering price reduction of $2 per wallet

- Considering hiring McKinsey for $250,000

First, Ming determines the *manufacturing sales price* (MSP), using the following formula:

$$MSP = P_r - M_r - M_w$$

Where

P_r = retail price
M_r = retail margin percentage
M_w = wholesale margin or mark-up

Now we just plug in the numbers:

$$MSP = \$10 - \$3 - \$.6 = \$6.40$$

Next, Ming calculates the *contribution per unit* (C_{pu}) based on this formula:

$$C_{pu} = MSP - P_v$$

Where

P_v = total variable price

This works out to:

$$C_{pu} = \$6.40 - \$3 = \$3.40$$

At this point, she starts the break-even sequence, beginning with *break-even volume*, using the formula:

$$BE = \frac{C_f}{C_{pu}}$$

Where

BE = break-even volume
C_f = total fixed costs

Ming plugs in the numbers as follows:

$$BE = \frac{\$1,800,000}{\$3.40} = 529,411 \text{ (wallets)}$$

She now wants to calculate her break-even volume, assuming the $2 reduction in price to see what the difference is between the two break-even figures. She uses the following formula:

$$BE_\Delta = \left(\frac{\text{Original } C_{pu}}{\text{New } C_{pu}}\right) \times \text{Original BE}$$

Where

BE_Δ = breakeven volume *after* price change
Original C_{pu} = $3.40
New C_{pu} = $1.40
Original BE = 529,411

This comes to:

$$BE_\Delta = \left(\frac{\$3.40}{\$1.40}\right) \times 529,411 = 1,285,712$$

Lowering the price by $2 has a significant impact on the break-even figures. Ming then focuses on determining *break-even market share* using the formula:

$$BE_{ms} = \frac{BE}{TM}$$

Where

BE_{ms} = break-even market share
BE = 529,411
TM = 35,000,000

This is calculated as follows:

$$BE_{ms} = \frac{529,411}{35,000,000} = 1.5\%$$

Ming also decides to calculate break-even market share assuming the price reduction, with this result:

$$BE_{ms} = \frac{1,285,712}{35,000,000} = 3.6\%$$

Finally, Ming wants to know break-even when it includes the cost of hiring McKinsey. So she figures break-even when including the investment for McKinsey (BE_{fc}) as follows:

$$BE_{fc} = \frac{C_f}{C_{pu}}$$

$$BE_{fc} = \frac{\$250,000}{\$3.40} = 73,529$$

Therefore, Ming would need to sell another 73,529 wallets to cover the added cost of McKinsey.

This alternative analysis shows the different ways to look at determining break-even. In both of these approaches, you can see the importance of understanding the costs involved in acquiring customers. A good way to use both is to determine the various break-even levels as demonstrated in the second approach, then factor in the marketing costs, customer retention and customer response rates to provide an in-depth analysis that is sure to impress the board and also provide guidance on the various goal measures needed to achieve success.

What it Means and Potential Challenges

It goes without saying that this analysis helps determine when you will break even and what the various influences are on the final calculations. In describing break-even, I have the advantage of plugging in readily available numbers. You may find that a fair amount of research is needed to collect the right numbers since your organization may not measure things consistently or use the same terms I applied here. But reliable numbers are important, to the extent that you can get them. They will give your analysis and marketing recommendations added credibility, so that you avoid the scourge of so many other marketers who proffer adjective-laden promises of glory, but with little analytical validity to support their giddiness. This, in particular, is one reason why marketers are often derided — because they do not take the final step to translate their enthusiasm into believable business objectives that non-marketers would find compelling.

On the flip-side, even with this analysis, you will not be right, nor are these formulas prescriptive. The analysis merely gives you an added sense of the conditions needed to achieve break-even. You, your team, your sales people, indeed your entire company, have to actually make it happen. No amount of analysis will make the customer transactions occur. That is why I offer the qualitative measures in this book as well, because both are needed to have a better chance of success.

[1] Loyalty/Survival Factors:
Year 1 = $.90^0$ = 1
Year 2 = $.90^1$ = .9
Year 3 = $.90^2$ = .81
Year 4 = $.90^3$ = .729
Year 5 = $.90^4$ = .656

[2] Year 1 = $.45^0$ = 1
Year 2 = $.45^1$ = .45
Year 3 = $.45^2$ = .2
Year 4 = $.45^3$ = .091
Year 5 = $.45^4$ = .041

Lifetime Value of Customer (LTVC)

Similar to customer acquisition and break-even, lifetime value has multiple approaches which are variations on an overall theme: assessing the value of a given customer over the lifetime of his or her relationship with your company. The academic research on this topic is extensive and deep and the more sophisticated formulas would make a particle physicist jealous. They include a range of components such as NPV (net present value...you calculate this to find out the time-adjusted value of money), stochastic models and Iso-value curves (a way of graphically depicting the customers and their future values despite past behavioral differences). For your sake and mine, I will describe two simplified approaches here, recognizing that they are shorthand approaches. Should you wish a more detailed treatment of LTVC, I encourage you to review research from Peter S. Fader and David C. Schmittlein, both of The Wharton School; Bruce G.S. Hardie, of the London Business School; and Elie Ofek, from Harvard Business School, among many others.

Furthermore, there are many online calculators that will enable you to determine LTVC. Here are links to two of them:

http://www.zeromillion.com/marketing/determining-lifetimevalue.html
http://hbswk.hbs.edu/item.jhtml?id=1436&t=marketing

Approach 1

THE DEFINITION

LTVC is a basic formula that estimates the dollar value (typically, the flow of profits) of a customer's long-term relationship with a company. It is a way of measuring how much a customer is worth over that span of time. I have adapted from marketingprofs.com as it provides a simplified and reasonable approach to LTVC.

THE FORMULA AND ITS COMPONENTS

First, let's get familiar with the terms:

M = average amount of money spent per purchase
C = average costs to service each purchase
P = number of purchases per year
Y = number of years you expect to keep this customer
A = new-customer acquisition cost
N = number of new customers referred by original customer
F = customer adjustment factor, which is applied to the period of time being evaluated. 1 is considered steady state, so no correction is needed. You may question the purpose of the correction factor. The correction factor captures changes you expect, or consider likely to happen, in a customer's behavior over a given period of time. For example, if you forecast that the customer will *increase* the amount they spend on each purchase or visit over time (perhaps because you assume you will cultivate their loyalty), then increase the size of the correction factor. Conversely, if you estimate the customer will *decrease* their spending over time, then factor in a lower number such as .9 or .8. This obviously depends on your insight into that customer's behavior. Again, this highlights the importance of including both qualitative and quantitative measures in your analysis.

Next, the terms are grouped into individual equations.

M – C = The average gross profit generated by the customer per visit.
P × Y = Total number of visits over the customer's lifetime
A × N = The amount of money saved by the customer's referral

Putting this together, we can determine the lifetime value of the customers using the formula:

$$LTVC = [(M - C) \times (P \times Y) - A + (A \times N)] \times F$$

WHERE'S THE DATA?

The data is found in several areas. If you are a retailer, then the average customer-spending information can be found in scanner data simply by adding together total purchases and dividing by the number of customers, or transactions, depending on how sophisticated your point-of-purchase system is. Average costs can be found in your income statement or your daily bookkeeping records. The forecast numbers are estimates, based either on historical experience, industry benchmarks or perhaps even new services, products or technologies that you believe influence customers' buying patterns. The customer-acquisition costs have already been discussed in the previous sections. Finding out accurately the number of new customers a customer refers to your company requires a fair amount of individual customer knowledge and/or a customer-relationship manager or even a basic database designed to track these kinds of activities. The correction factor is as much a guess as anything. But if you know your business or have a sense of how competitors perform, then you should be able to estimate a reasonable correction factor.

CALCULATING IT

In calculating LTVC, I will use the figures from the break-even analysis used in Magic Number 31 (Ravi's Amazing Auto Parts, regular customers, acquired list) for the sake of consistency and simplicity. I will also make basic assumptions for the other costs.

- Average spent per purchase: $30

- Average costs to service each purchase: $2 (this reflects the transaction charges and any contact time the customer may have with support, either live or online…this is generalized and does not attempt to adjust for the typically lower cost of online support vis-à-vis live support)

- Number of purchases per year: three

- Number of years you expect to keep this customer: 20

- New-customer acquisition cost: $0.60

- Number of new customers referred by original customer: four

- Customer adjustment factor for the time period analyzed: 1.2 (reviewing earlier descriptions, this means that the customer is likely to increase the amount he or she purchases from you over time. A correction factor of less than 1 would indicate that the customer would spend a lower amount each time).

We plug these values into the equation and get the following:

$$[(\$30 - \$2) \times (3 \times 20) - \$0.60 + (\$0.60 \times 4)] \times 1.2 = \$2{,}018$$

Thus, the LTVC of a regular customer from an acquired list for Ravi is $2,018. Considering that the average purchase price is $30, you can appreciate the importance of developing long-term relationships with customers because that first purchase, if handled thoughtfully, can lead to many years of returns for Ravi. The converse is true as well. Mishandling that first purchase will mean Ravi loses nearly $2,000 in long-term potential value.

The conclusion is clear: the development of customer relationships must be taken seriously. Equally clear is that once you have outlined the performance metrics, you still need to instill the proper qualitative behaviors in your staff to realize the long-term value. Do not assume that running the numbers will make the relationship happen. The challenge to running a successful business is knowing how to translate the numbers into inspiration that drives performance.

Approach 2

THE DEFINITION

The definition remains the same.

THE FORMULA AND ITS COMPONENTS

This formula requires knowing your contribution per unit, which we have already reviewed in Magic Number 14. Furthermore, you must make certain assumptions about the annual (natural) rate of customer attrition (a variation on retention) and the discount rate. The discount rate is the percentage used to calculate net present value, which helps you determine the time value of money. Estimating the discount rate is important. It usually has two parts: a risk-adjusted return on the use of that money, and some sort of adjustment for inflation.

WHERE'S THE DATA?

Without making you lose your mind by tossing even more complexity into this stew, the discount rate is often tied to a more conventional reference rate. In the U.S., this can include 30-year Treasury notes, for example. Peter Temple, in his book *Magic Numbers: The 33 Key Ratios That Every Investor Should Know*, explains the discount rate as follows:

"Discount rate: this is the risk-free rate of return on ten-year money, which equates...to the yield to maturity on the benchmark ten-year government bond for the country in question. You can add in an equity risk premium. Data on equity risk premiums are sketchy. The long-term average for the U.K. is said to be 5.2%. You should probably use a minimum of 3% for even the least volatile stocks. If the yield on the ten-year bond is, say, 4% and the risk premium used is 5%, the discount rate would be 9% (4+5)." (pp.186–187)

CALCULATING IT

For now, let's assume your discount rate is 9%. You also need your estimated customer-attrition rate (or the inverse of the retention rate). I'll use 10% in this case. First, you should calculate the *net discount rate*, a key component of this approach to calculating LTVC.

$$\text{Net discount rate} = \frac{(r + a)}{(1 - r)}$$

Where

r = the discount rate
a = the attrition rate

Once again, you merely plug in the numbers:

$$\text{Net discount rate} = \frac{(.09 + .10)}{(1 - .05)} = 2\%$$

The net discount rate is then included in this approach's LTVC formula, which is

$$LTVC = \frac{C_{pu}}{1 - \dfrac{1}{(1 + \text{net discount rate})}}$$

I'll make the assumption that your product's C_{pu} is \$5 in this example.

This works out to

$$LTVC = \frac{\$5}{1 - \dfrac{1}{(1 + .2)}} = \$29.99$$

Effectively, the LTVC per unit is around \$30 for this customer.

Simplified Example

One of the companies I started was a hotel firm. We used an even simpler approach to communicate the value of customers because we wanted to convey the essence of the total value a given guest represented. This exercise is not original, as it has been applied in other businesses, but it is powerful nevertheless.

We would ask new members of our staff how much a guest was worth when he or she first walked through the front door. The answers varied, but they were usually based on the price of an average room, plus the average money spent on a meal in our restaurant. As we asked new employees attending our training sessions to reply, they usually said things like "\$200" or "\$150" or, in the case of the really bold, "\$300". We would then tell them it was closer to \$55,000. They were shocked and surprised. Then we explained that, if the guest enjoyed their stay, they would visit us twice a year for at least 10 years and would also tell five other people, 20% of whom would stay with us as well. Hopefully, when these folks stayed with us, a similar dynamic would occur.

Leaving out the more rigorous mathematical permutations and adjustments for frequency, discounts and so forth, we would then walk through the calculations for our staff:

- Average room rate: $150 (that was our ADR, or average daily rate)

- Average length of stay: two nights

- Average food and beverage: $200 (two dinners and a breakfast)

- Twice per year for 10 years.

The length of stay, number of visits and lifetime tenure figures were based on industry averages in our region at the time.

This would amount to a rough figure of $10,000 just for that couple (most of our guests were couples because our main property was a mountain resort, not a business traveler hotel).

We then factored in the five additional people that guest would tell of their positive experience, and which ultimately led to one of those five also staying at our hotel for the same period of time and with the same conditions. We assumed that this couple would stay with us in the year following the first couple's stay. This amount equaled $9,000 over the remaining years of the first couple's 10-year period. The next couple told would be valued at $8,000 for the remaining eight years of the first couple's tenure, and so on.

Yes, you can already see the flaws in this approach. First, we did not account for the full 10-year relationships for each of the subsequent couples. We also did not calculate the other potential couples each of those couples might tell. But you get the idea, as did our staff. If nothing else, the $55,000 figure *underestimated* the lifetime value of our guests.

Finally, to drive home the importance to our staff that each guest was worth a great deal as a long-term annuity or revenue stream, and to reinforce positive service behavior, we tied performance bonuses to guest satisfaction in which an employee could earn 30% of their base wages in end-of-year bonus for outstanding guest performance. We based performance on repeat guests, increased occupancy, length of stay, amount spent per stay, average daily rate and qualitative measures such as how guests viewed the hotel and whether they made reference to the good service of specific people.

There was another reason we described the importance of lifetime value. By focusing on superior service, we believed that we could earn greater loyalty, but not just over a 10-year period. We hoped to increase the length of stay for each individual visit. When we took over the resort, the average length of stay was one night. By focusing on great service, we hoped to persuade guests to stay longer. Even increasing our average length of stay for all guests to 1.5 nights meant a 50% increase in revenues. Fortunately, we achieved this and ended up doubling revenues in the first year alone.

What it Means and Potential Challenges

Lifetime value in these approaches can be influenced by what data is used and how it is interpreted. For example, determining the average spending per customer is dependent on whether you are using transactions or customers in your calculation. If you are adding together total purchases and dividing by the number of transactions, then you may be under-representing the value of some customers since their separate multiple purchases would be viewed purely as if they were separate customers. On the other hand, accurately determining actual customer purchases requires a more sophisticated tool which not all retailers may have, such as loyalty cards that can be scanned with each purchase. Furthermore, loyalty cards (in this case) may not be used consistently by customers, which can skew the analysis.

Cost figures are quite challenging to determine at the individual purchase level. Are you measuring the cost of the entire operation at the time the customer made his or her purchase? Or are you assessing the costs specific to that transaction? If you are measuring the costs specific to the transaction, you will find those are very hard to determine with any degree of precision. Therefore, it is most useful if you determine a set of costs that are normal for each operation and that are applicable to customer-specific transactions, then consistently apply these every time you measure costs.

As I have mentioned several times in this book, there is no single formula that is perfect and the same is true with LTVC. Even with the more sophisticated modeling mentioned at the beginning of this section, you must be comfortable knowing that your customers simply will not behave according to your predictions. This is similar to the economic theory that assumes a rational customer. It is convenient from a modeling and analytical point of view, but it does not reflect the nuances of day-to-day consumer behavior. Despite your best efforts, LTVC will be a guide only.

Part Four

MAGIC NUMBERS FOR UNDERSTANDING MARKETING

MAGIC NUMBERS FOR UNDERSTANDING MARKETING

While this entire book deals with marketing, this section concentrates on measuring specific activities within marketing. From the return on investment for marketing to specific measures of retail transactions performance, each enables companies to better understand the results from their marketing programs.

PRICING MEASURES

Pricing is an important marketing tool as it is an indicator of value, positioning and substitutability. Marketers have several ways to measure pricing decisions and each depends on their overall strategic marketing objectives for the products and services under consideration. The main pricing measures we will discuss are:

- Price
- Premiums
- Marketing ROI (floor pricing)
- Mark-up price
- Target-return price
- Profit-maximizing price.

MAGIC NUM8ER

33

Price

THE DEFINITION

This is the amount of money you charge for a product or service.

THE FORMULA AND ITS COMPONENTS

$$P = PL - D - A - T$$

Where

P   = price (the final price realized)
PL = list price (your target full retail price)
D   = discounts (percentage reduction from list price, usually based on volume)
A   = allowances (price reductions issued for trade-ins and/or promotional dollars from cooperative marketing activities between the manufacturer and retailer)
T   = taxes

WHERE'S THE DATA?

Pricing data should come from your business and sales plans for each product. Often, sales representatives control final price, usually within pre-set guidelines, because they are dealing directly with the customer at the point of sale and know firsthand what the customer is seeking. Of course, as each order comes in from the market, this information is fed directly into your company's financial reports, where the details of each transaction are fully described. Sales people should be recording the final agreed price and quantity figures accurately so that your accountants know how to categorize the price specifics (i.e. depending on your company's accounting practices, you may count allowances and discounts against marketing's programs budget, or you may count them against the sales team directly, especially if you are measuring individual sales representatives' performance based on profitability; or it may be a combination of these methods).

CALCULATING IT

Let's go back to Ming's Squeezer wallet business from Magic Number 10 and look a bit more closely to see what her actual pricing is relative to her retail price target of $10. As it turns out, Ming has developed marketing and sales programs to encourage her retailers to buy the Squeezer. Taxes are those imposed by the national and local taxing authorities. Tariffs are generally international charges imposed on the import of goods. In Ming's case, this amounts to 5%. The programs include:

- Discounts that average 5%

- Allowances that average 2%

P = $10 − $0.50 − $0.20 − $0.50 = $8.80

Therefore, you can see that her list price of $10 nets out to $8.80 per wallet sold.

WHAT IT MEANS AND POTENTIAL CHALLENGES

Outlining each of the components of price reveals a sizable impact on profitability, since the gross revenues do not count these figures. Seeing price this way also serves to assist Ming in determining future product direction, pricing and customer demand, for many reasons. First, if her $10 list price is generally acceptable, and her various pricing programs are embraced by retailers, then Ming will logically conclude that her pricing is viewed as favorable in the market, which would influence her future product decisions. However, it is quite possible that Ming may have missed important market opportunities with her pricing scheme. If her goal, and that of her company, is to increase market share, then a more aggressive pricing approach would have been warranted. Any and each of the price components described could have been altered to encourage demand: lower list price, higher discounts to inspire the retailer to buy larger quantities, higher allowances to encourage more promotion and support from the retailer…you get the idea. Ming has less control over taxes and tariffs, but does need to factor them into her final pricing analysis and recommendations. If her goal was to maximize profit and position the Squeezer as a premium product in the wallet category, then it is possible she under-priced it and left some profits on the table. We will look at profit-maximizing pricing in Magic Number 38.

On a strategic level, price is more than a simple equation as described here. Companies must consider their positioning, financial growth and share objectives in weighing pricing decisions. Typically, a pricing strategy will include considering whether your objectives are volume objectives, profit objectives or some other set of considerations such as competitive parity. If volume is your objective, then you are considering financial, unit and/or market share growth. Penetration pricing is one possible approach in this case. This means you set price low enough to capture rapid market share. It is most often used when competitors have identical, similar or better products to yours. If your objective is profitability, then a skimming pricing strategy is most often used. This means that a company believes its product offering is unique and innovative and, consequently, has a probable lead over competitors with its new product. Therefore, companies set price at a premium level, both to capture higher profits and to establish a market-leading position. Over time, the price can be reduced as competition enters (which it will inevitably do, since competitors will notice a company's success and want to get their share of it as well). Magic Numbers 36–38 will cover useful pricing formulas designed to achieve differing objectives:

- Mark-up pricing: whether a company's objective is volume or profit, mark-up pricing is a tool that enables the firm to earn a reasonable profit based on its strategic goals. Of course, as with most pricing and marketing formulas, this is directly influenced by the accuracy of each firm's estimates.

- Target-return pricing: this approach helps a firm determine price based on its return-on-investment objectives for a given product or project. Again, this can apply to volume or profit strategies.

- Profit-maximizing pricing: achieving a prescribed profitability level is the focus of this approach. It tends to be more useful for a profit-centered strategy, although one can reasonably argue that even a volume strategy requires a profit objective, just simply on a different scale and positioning objective.

Marketing managers are not limited to these approaches. It is quite possible that a blended approach may be the most sensible, whereby a firm chooses to price mid market. This decision, however, must be considered in the context of a firm's overall positioning objectives. Often, a middle approach can become no-man's land in which the products are not perceived as either premium or mass market. Consequently, the consumer does not know what the product stands for. If a reasonable benefits argument for this middle approach cannot be made, then consumers are likely to buy on the basis of either cheapest cost or most unique features.

Premiums

THE DEFINITION

There are two "premiums" I will define here. As you will see, there are minor contradictions between them.

Marketing's definition 1: *"a product with a marketing slogan, message or brand name on it that is used as a giveaway to prospective customers in the hope that it will attract their business."* Promotional items come in thousands of insignificant products, designs and styles — coffee mugs, pens, t-shirts, post-it pads, mouse pads, glow sticks, magnetic business cards. They're cheap to produce and that's why they're giveaways.

Marketing's definition 2: price premium. A price premium is the price you can charge above normal price as a result of any of a number of factors: strong brand name, superior quality or performance, unique features and so forth…

THE FORMULA AND ITS COMPONENTS

Premium does not have a specific formula. Magic Number 38, Profit-maximizing Price, is a reasonable starting point for this price-premium definition. But there is more to premium than just setting a profit-maximizing price. Marketers must have information that describes consumers' perceptions of their brand, preferably in comparison to competitors' brands. These perceptions can indicate if your brand is considered to be of higher or lower value than a competitor's, helping you better gauge your price premium flexibility. Factoring in reputation, perceived quality and relative market position will further sharpen your understanding of your brand's premium position. But recognize that these are often qualitative assessments, with interpretation and judgment as guides, so perfect precision in determining premium price is not attainable.

WHERE'S THE DATA?

While many pricing models are influenced by costs, premiums are affected more by brand equity and overall brand value (see Magic Numbers 18 and 19), each of which affect and create their brand perception. Specifically, the value of your brand directly affects the credibility associated with the premium you charge. Mercedes and BMW can charge a price premium for their cars because their brand is consistently associated with a higher perceived value. Whether your premium is a mark-up from competing products because of its added value or it is a promotional giveaway or discounted offering, brand equity and brand value affect your choice of approach. At the extreme, Saturn (from General Motors) is unlikely to have any credibility if it were to introduce a premium-priced car since this would be inconsistent with its image. Lexus was launched as a new brand, and not as part of Toyota, in part due to the association Toyota generally had with entry-level and mid-market cars.

CALCULATING IT

Calculating price premiums is based on a number of factors, as already stated. Does the firm have brand equity such that its brand is perceived as being of higher quality than its competitors? What are the target customers' perceptions of your brand? In other words, your brand equity may be higher than the competition, but you may also be in a period of decline brought about by recent problems, as a result of which brand equity has not yet caught up with the reduction in perceived added value.

WHAT IT MEANS AND POTENTIAL CHALLENGES

A simple question arises from these two definitions: does "premium" connote a high-value product at a premium price, or is it a promo item to be given away? The answer? Both!

This Magic Number is closely connected with Magic Numbers 20, Brand Equity, and 21, Brand name Premium (where "premium" is defined as a price strategy). Some of the luxury brands mentioned in this book pursue a pricing strategy known as "skimming", which means charging the highest possible price for uniqueness or innovation relative to current substitutes. Skimming strategies are targeted to exclusive, high-end markets only, where there is a sufficient number of customers to sustain the business but not so many as to attract competitors. Products with a superior image and reputation can be good candidates for skimming. Skimming pricing helps convey and reinforce a strong brand-name premium and, overall, can help drive superior brand equity.

Let's look at a few examples.

Rolex

As we saw earlier, Rolex is widely considered a top-quality watch. An interesting aspect to Rolex is that its components (the mechanisms that make the watch work) are very similar to those used in other watch brands, whether at the luxury or commodity ends of the spectrum. I do not know the specific percentage of gold, diamonds and other precious materials used in the construction of a Rolex, but it is highly unlikely that the aggregate value of these components when compared against the aggregate value of standard, non-precious components is in the range of thousands of dollars. So what are Rolex customers buying? They are buying prestige, image, tradition, reputation and even association with a socio-demographic audience that is among the top 1% of income earners.

How has Rolex been so successful in capturing this audience and in convincing them that its watches are worth the money? Certainly, Rolexes do have a reputation for quality (except for those "Rolexes" found in the night markets of Bangkok). This has been true for decades. We never read about quality-control issues or product recalls from Rolex. Concomitant with quality is implied expertise in workmanship. Rolex does seem to have figured out over the years how to build an extremely reliable watch with almost-flawless components. Therefore, it is reasonably safe to assume that its reputation for quality is deserved. But does that justify its premium image? Let's look deeper. Rolex has been the favorite of "ultra-successful" people for years. This either suggests that ultra-successful people have been part of a multi-decade dupe (and are, by extension, despite their success, quite gullible) or that they believe in Rolex's promise of quality, find its high-status image appealing, and are not disappointed by the product once they use it.

Clearly, quality is part of Rolex's premium, but so is its reputation for being worn by the most discriminating customers. Does that warrant its premium image? It helps. Psychologically, people like to associate with others like them, and/or aspire to be like other people whom they perceive as being successful. Rolex's customers get a psychological reward for wearing a Rolex. But beyond quality and discriminating customers, there are still other factors that contribute to Rolex's premium image: tradition, brand associations (golf, yachts, luxury cars…) that serve to reinforce the reputation. While, separately, each of these may not justify Rolex's premium image, it is these ingredients collectively that create the premium image the company enjoys. The challenge, of course, is how to maintain this image.

Most of the great luxury brands took years to develop their reputations. Four Seasons, Rolex, Cunard, Rolls Royce…all own a well-honed image in the market. In many ways, these products are considered one of a kind. It requires tremendous focus, dedication and a clear understanding of the company's purpose and heritage to be able to uphold these values consistently, especially in difficult business conditions. Furthermore, despite the tradition associated with many luxury products, tradition alone will not sustain them for long. There is a fair amount of rigorous work that goes into the details of the product. The service at Cunard or Four Seasons is the result of years of training of employees, devotion to mission, a clear understanding of customers and a commitment to retaining employees who understand all of this. Similarly, the prestige associated with Rolls Royce and Rolex is the result of dedication to first-rate quality. The bottom line is that these firms are passionately committed to protecting their reputations, retaining the absolute loyalty of their customers and maintaining the mystique of their products. It is part of their corporate cultural DNA.

Now let's look at an example of marketing's other definition of "premium", which relates to an added "value" to influence the purchase of a product. Crudely, banks used to offer a free appliance (such as a toaster) as a premium or incentive to attract new customers. The appliance cost the banks little *if* a customer actually opened an account, but was a cost drain initially because there wasn't always a one-to-one relationship between the number of appliances acquired upfront and the number of new customers who opened an account directly as a result of the offer. Nevertheless, this premium served to bring in customers. More recent examples include video-game consoles and bundled games. The product to be sold is the console, but the bundled games are the premium added to encourage purchase. Of course, the games are rarely the most popular games. But the premium often works in these instances because a customer acquires the console and receives a free game, realizes the fun involved in playing and returns to the retailer to buy more games. The company effectively creates a form of annuity, assuming the customer is a dedicated gamer. The reason is simple: the premium game inspired the purchase of the console; playing the console then inspired the purchase of more games; as new games are subsequently introduced, the customer's desire for these grows as well and leads to more purchases. Premium, in these examples, can be viewed as a way to attract "premium customers" — that is, customers who become loyal to the product or company. The challenge, of course, is forecasting demand accurately enough to "know" that you are paying for the cost of the premium you are including.

Finally, as mentioned above, a price premium captures the higher price paid by customers as recognition of the product's premium image. However, price premium is tricky, for the same reasons that sustaining a premium image is challenging overall. It is very hard to actually know if the desired price is going to be the price ultimately charged at the time of purchase. Any discount below full price risks diluting and undermining the brand image. Yet not selling the product at all risks undermining the company's survival. Interestingly, there is no single hard-and-fast rule when it comes to price premium. It is hard to think of an instance when there has been a Rolex "sale", yet Mercedes and BMW regularly offer financing or even direct-from-sticker discounts (despite their luxury positions). Each of these companies attracts high-end customers and each has been largely successful in maintaining its image over time. But clearly each would suffer if a prolonged program of price discounting were enacted.

Cunard[1] confronted this in the early 1990s following the first Gulf War. At the time, Cunard operated seven ships, five of which were five-star vessels and the other two four-star. Their premier ship was the Queen Elizabeth II, more commonly known as the QE2. Cunard had 50% of the five-star market but, for the first time in its 160-year history, it was facing dwindling demand and competitive discounting. Customers traveling on a Cunard ship expected and received an extraordinarily high level of service. However, increasing evidence suggested that the culture of cruising was changing and passengers were finding the more family-oriented atmosphere of the emerging cruise lines to be attractive. Cunard wrestled with this and responded by offering premiums, effectively discounting their original service. These premiums came in several forms: a shopping spree at Harrod's; travel on the Concorde; reduced fares for the second passenger; and even a one-day sale. Fast forward to today and Cunard no longer operates the four-star ships and focuses exclusively on five-star, ultra-luxury, cruising with the newly launched Queen Mary and the QE2. Sometime during the past decade Cunard concluded that protecting its prestigious upper-class legacy was more important than chasing the discounted four-star and family-cruise approaches.

[1] Young, Robert F., Greyser, Stephen A., "Cunard Line Ltd.: Managing Integrated Communications Case # 9-594-046 ©1994 The President and Fellows of Harvard College.

35 Marketing ROI (floor price)

THE DEFINITION

Marketing ROI describes the return on a company's marketing investment. Broadly speaking, this is analogous to financial ROI and helps you determine the total return on the marketing dollars you invest.[1]

There are a few variations on this analysis, two of which I will show here and a third was discussed in Magic Number 25, Segment Profitability. The first reflects the more classic finance approach and is explained in greater depth in Magic Number 29, Customer Investment.

For illustration, I will focus on the second formula, which is ROI based on a concept called "cost-based floor price". This type of ROI analysis focuses on the cost of a given product and the expected or desired margin (profit) that you hope to achieve.

THE FORMULAS

Classic ROI

$$ROI = \frac{P_n}{A_t}$$

Where

P_n = net profit
A_t = total assets

Cost-based ROI

$$ROI = \frac{V \times P - V \times C_u - E_m - E_o}{I}$$

Where

V = volume
P = price
C_u = unit cost
E_m = manufacturing expense
E_o = operating expense
I   = investment required to achieve ROI targets

Where's the Data?

The data is derived from the income statement in your firm's financial reports. Typically, you will find several costs described, including manufacturing and operating expenses.

Calculating It

To illustrate cost-based ROI, I will use hypothetical numbers from Nike. The scenario and figures are similar to those a product marketing manager at Nike might encounter.

- Asian factory with five million pairs per year production or manufacturing capacity.

- Nike expects to sell five million pairs per year; knowing the expected quantity, the factory tells Nike it can produce the shoes for $20 per pair.

- Fixed expense (the total annual charges from the factory for rent, wages…) is $10 million.

- Nike expects a 45% ROI. Anything less and it won't go forward with the product.

- Operating expenses are $10,000,000.

- Investment of $30,000,000.

These assumptions provide the necessary components to calculate ROI:

$$.45 = \frac{\$5,000,000 \times P - \$5,000,000 \times \$20 - \$10,000,000 - \$10,000,000}{\$30,000,000}$$

$$.45 = \frac{\$1,000,000P - \$1,000,000 \times \$20 - \$2,000,000 - \$2,000,000}{\$6,000,000}$$

$\$6,000,000 \times .45 = \$1,000,000P - \$24,000,000$

$\$2,700,000 = \$1,000,000P - \$24,000,000$

$\$26,700,000 = \$1,000,000P$

$\$26.70 = P$

Therefore, \$26.70 is the "floor price" Nike should charge to achieve its pre-tax ROI of 45%.

What it Means and Potential Challenges

The main challenge is that the floor price has no bearing on market demand, competition factors or what customers would be willing to pay. Furthermore, this approach to ROI is not an effective method for determining the best price, only the minimum price needed to achieve the ROI target. If customers decide that Nike's price is too high, then the desired ROI won't be met. Another challenge to this and other ROI measures (a third measure is net income divided by total assets) is that it accounts only for tangible assets. Yet each company's value is partly derived from the values of the brand or product name itself, the customer relationships, the ideas bouncing around inside the heads of its employees (a form of future potential value), partners and even its historical traditions. ROI measures do not account for these increasingly recognized key contributors to the overall value of the company.

---

[1] A more sophisticated treatment of ROI would include a net present value (NPV) analysis, which would help determine the length of time before the investment pays off. This includes knowledge about discount rates and time periods.

MAGIC NUM8ER

36

Mark-Up Price

THE DEFINITION

This is a basic pricing method that adds a slight increase, or "mark-up", to the product's cost. It is often used in professional-service businesses. My own company has employed this method occasionally. In effect, we calculate our base costs to complete a project, then add a mark-up of x% to reflect the premium we believe our services represented.

THE FORMULA AND ITS COMPONENTS

$$\text{Mark-up price} = \frac{\text{unit cost}}{(1 - \text{expected return on sales})}$$

Obviously, you need to determine unit cost to calculate the mark-up pricing formula. To do that, use this formula:

$$\text{Unit cost} = \text{variable cost} + \frac{\text{fixed costs}}{\text{unit sales}}$$

WHERE'S THE DATA?

Mark-up pricing is based on estimates of the total costs for a project or product and, therefore, the data can be found in the company's marketing plans and accounting budgets for each department. Identifying the costs is the tricky part, so a company's systems must be sophisticated enough to measure cost inputs, both fixed and variable, to the unit level. Once the costs are known, or estimated, then the marketing manager's job is to identify a reasonable mark-up price. This is most likely driven by the company's strategic margin goals for each product line, as well as the positioning goals for each product in each product line. The reason for noting the positioning goals is that pricing has a direct impact on consumers' perceptions of a product's position vis-à-vis the competition.

Finance and/or accounting will have information on specific fixed costs allocated to your department. As with all numbers that describe or affect your marketing decisions, you should double-check accounting's figures against your own budget figures to see what differences there are, if any. Usually, the accountants have specific rules that govern how to count certain costs and these tend to be more detailed than the more basic budgets marketing departments (or most other departments, for that matter) would submit. It is quite likely that your figures will not match the figures from accounting or finance, but that is probably as a consequence of these rules.

CALCULATING IT

Professional-service firms often use mark-up pricing by estimating the total project cost, then adding in their profit, or mark-up. My firm, Brand New View, for example, has a set of daily fees based on the type of project involved, typically several thousand dollars. This fee is really the minimum cost of entry for customers. At that point, different levels of customization dictate our mark-up, as well as whether travel and other factors are involved. The total fees go toward paying salaries for the principals, covering the costs for time investment, administrative overhead and materials fees (such as when we use third-party cases in our executive-education programs, and also the base costs for binders, handouts, et al).

Manufacturing operations have a similar approach that requires understanding certain key costs and sales estimates to calculate a cost per unit, from which the mark-up price can ultimately be determined.

In the following case, Sujiyo runs a manufacturing company, Tzetumuch, which makes sumo *mawashis* (the little belts worn by sumos that leave little to the imagination). The following are his expected costs and financials:

- Variable costs $15
- Fixed costs $200,000
- Expected sales $40,000

Sujiyo positions his *mawashis* at the premium end of the market (because they are made out of silk), so while his costs are slightly higher than his commodity-like competitors, his *mawashis* command high prices because they feel comfortable and look nice. Therefore, he expects a mark-up of 20%. His pricing can now be calculated.

First, we determine unit cost:

$$\text{Unit cost} = \text{variable cost} + \frac{\text{fixed costs}}{\text{unit sales}}$$

$$\text{Unit cost} = \$15 + \frac{\$200,000}{\$40,000} = \$20$$

Next, we add this figure into the mark-up price equation

$$\text{Mark-up price} = \frac{\text{unit cost}}{(1 - \text{expected return on sales})}$$

$$\text{Mark-up price} = \frac{\$20}{(1 - 0.2)} = \$25$$

Sujiyo's mark-up price to his retail accounts is $25. His profit is $5 on each *mawashi* he sells. His dealers will likely mark up the *mawashi* again since they too want to make a profit. In many apparel markets, a mark-up term known as "keystone pricing" is used and it typically means a 50% increase above the manufacturer's price. So Sujiyo's dealers would sell his *mawashis* for $37.50.

What it Means and Potential Challenges

Mark-up pricing is generally a simple, yet not the most effective, approach to pricing. It is simple because you only need to estimate the mark-up you wish to earn above cost, and price accordingly. It is not always effective because you may not be maximizing your profit or sales potential. Perhaps the customer sees Sujiyo's *mawashis* as being of only mediocre value, despite the fine silk material. If so, Sujiyo is unlikely to hit his sales target. On the other hand, customers may perceive them as being extraordinary value at $37.50. Sujiyo then has to wonder whether he would sell just as many if the price were $5 or $10 higher, thereby improving his margins.

While mark-up pricing is simple, since it is really based on covering costs plus adding a little margin, it may leave out any unique positioning opportunities that could help you build a more reputable, exclusive brand. Even if your goal is not to be a high-end brand, you may still be leaving money on the table.

Target–Return Price

THE DEFINITION

This method is designed to cover all costs and yield a specified or target return. Like mark-up pricing, it is another cost-based approach.

THE FORMULA AND ITS COMPONENTS

$$TRP = \frac{C_{pu} + R \times I}{S_u}$$

Where

TRP = target-return price
C_{pu} = cost per unit
R = expected return
I = capital invested
S_u = unit sales

WHERE'S THE DATA?

The data is in the usual place — most likely your finance and accounting department. Since one of the formula's variables is "capital invested", it is in your financial reports, specifically in the balance sheet under liabilities, either as shareholders' equity or long-term debt.

Unit sales are found, in their final form, in the income statement. However, since those are typically completed at the end of business cycles (quarterly, annually), preliminary figures can be found in sales or in the preliminary finance reports.

CALCULATING IT

Sujiyo's *mawashi* products are still selling well. Sojiyo wants to know what his target-return price would be by investing $500,000 in a *mawashi* fabric machine. Since he has positioned his *mawashis* as premium products and sells them at premium prices, he also has premium expectations on the return he expects for his $500,000 investment. Sujiyo decides he wants an ROI of 15%, which means he wants a price that would return $75,000.

Here's how his analysis looks:

$$\text{Target-return price} = 20 + \frac{.15 \times \$500,000}{\$40,000} = \$21.90$$

Therefore, his analysis reveals that if he wants a 15% ROI, he must set a target-return price of at least $21.90.

WHAT IT MEANS AND POTENTIAL CHALLENGES

Target-return pricing depends on the assumptions and expectations that went into it. For example, if your expected ROI is not in line with industry standards on similar projects, then it is quite possible that your target-return price will not adequately meet your needs. It is also conceivable that your unit sales assumptions are off, perhaps significantly. In this event, you would want to determine break-even at different sales volumes to see where a more accurate target-return price should be set. Keep in mind as well that target-return pricing ignores competitor pricing, customer response and market trends, all of which can affect the final analysis. As with other Magic Numbers, preparing multiple scenarios is often the key to selecting an approach with which you are most comfortable.

MAGIC NUM8ER 38

Pricing Frameworks

There are four additional pricing approaches that are more appropriately viewed as frameworks rather than as specific formulas.

Auction Pricing

THE DEFINITION

As with any auction, the price is not fixed, the product being placed in the market for buyers to bid. There are three types of auction pricing: Dutch, English and sealed-bid auctions. A Dutch auction is one in which the seller reduces the price until the buyer accepts it. By contrast, in an English auction, an item is sold to the highest bidder. Usually, items in an English auction are offered at a starting price from which the auctioneer, if it is a live auction, encourages the buyers to outbid each other. A sealed-bid auction is based on buyers submitting their bids directly to the seller. The seller then chooses the best bid among the many buyers. In the sealed-bid auction, the buyers only know their own bid and not those of their competitors.

THE FORMULA AND ITS COMPONENTS

There is no formula for this since auction pricing is more of a technique or a framework.

WHERE'S THE DATA?

Auction-pricing data is based on several factors: market knowledge of the item being sold and its equivalents, the perceived value of collectibles (information that is obtained often by years of study and informal knowledge sharing amongst a community of enthusiasts) and trends.

CALCULATING IT

Auction prices are determined by sellers in the form of a reserve price (also known as a "minimum price"), although products can be sold at auction without a minimum, should the seller so choose. Reserve prices are typically based on what the seller is willing to accept for the item and it may have little to do with current retail value and more to do with perceived or collectable value. Perceived value is driven by qualitative perceptions, either based on comparable pricing from similar products in the market or a common knowledge about the value of the item. Collectable value pertains to items that are assumed to be unique collector's items (art and antiques auctioned by Sotheby's and Christies, two leading auction houses that specialize in exclusive items, for example).

The company known as eBay, an online auction marketplace, is an excellent example of a company that uses English-auction pricing, as sellers list their products on eBay's website and buyers bid on the products until a satisfactory price is reached. Satisfaction is defined as the price at which the seller accepts the buyer's offer. eBay sellers often put a reserve price on their products and if no buyer reaches that price, then the product can be withdrawn by the seller. eBay has grown rapidly in the past several years and it offers a wide variety of products from automobiles to art to consumer collectibles.

WHAT IT MEANS AND POTENTIAL CHALLENGES

Auction pricing is an easy concept to understand. However, with the exception of some of the online marketplaces such as eBay, it is not commonly used in consumer marketing. While Sotheby's and Christies do use this technique, the items they auction are targeted to high-end, wealthy, consumers. It would be quite unusual to see a traditional retail store attempt auction pricing for buyers.

Value Pricing

THE DEFINITION

Value pricing is a practice employed by many large-scale retailers with in-house brands (also known as "store" brands). The objective is to offer consumers everyday low prices for high-quality products.

THE FORMULA AND ITS COMPONENTS

Again, there is no formula for this. Value pricing is perhaps easier to understand if it is described as an operating strategy, such as low-cost, since its success requires that a company have an excellent cost structure to ensure consistent profitability at lower prices.

WHERE'S THE DATA?

Value pricing requires intimate knowledge of your company's cost structure (to understand minimum price to recoup costs) and a clear strategy on margin goals. The data is also dependent on competitors' offerings and their price in equivalent channels in the marketplace.

CALCULATING IT

There is no specific calculation. Instead, a company must have a good understanding of its costs as well as knowledge of comparable products in the market to determine prices that attract more customers than the competitors.

WHAT IT MEANS AND POTENTIAL CHALLENGES

To be effective, a company must be willing to offer a good-quality product at a reasonable price. As mentioned, many of the large retailers do this with their in-house brands — WalMart from the U.S., Carrefour from France and IKEA from Sweden all practice value pricing. IKEA focuses on its own line of products and is able to offer value pricing by selling products unassembled, thus reducing its manufacturing costs and passing these savings on to customers. WalMart has a mix of in-house brands and well-known U.S. and international brands, selling them using value pricing. WalMart is able to sell branded products in this way because it is a dominant buyer and can negotiate significant discounts on products from manufacturers because of the sheer volume it purchases. The same is true for Carrefour.

Perceived-value Pricing

DEFINITION

This form of pricing is a bit trickier since it depends on a customer's perception of value, which can vary from customer to customer.

The Formula and its Components

There is no formula.

Where's the Data?

The data can be found through market research that reviews competitor data and customer needs. It is usually highly qualitative.

Calculating it

There is no calculation, either. However, a simple illustration will help demonstrate the concept. Suppose you are a toy maker that sells S$100,000 of toys per month directly through your website. An e-commerce software company demonstrates its product to you, which allows visitors to your website to buy products using a one-click shopping approach. (One-click is an online-shopping option that allows consumers to buy products by simply clicking the purchase button once rather than entering their complete data profile each time they purchase. This is accomplished by having customers set up online accounts with pre-approved credit cards for instant charging.) The e-commerce software company claims that using its software will enable you to increase your business by 40% since customers can purchase items more quickly and easily once they have set up their one-click account. Assuming that these claims are accurate, this would mean that you could increase business by $40,000 per month, The perceived value of the e-commerce software would be $40,000 and, at that price or below, you would probably be motivated to buy this software. If the price of the software were more than $40,000, then you would need to assess whether the additional money was worth it. Since the software could potentially produce a 40% change every month, then a price even slightly higher than $40,000 might be worthwhile. At some point, however, the price of the software could reach an unattractive level. So the challenge is in identifying the best perceived-value price.

What it Means and Potential Challenges

Perceived-value pricing, while hard to reduce to a common formula, is quite powerful and found in numerous consumer-product categories around the world. Perceived value influences how much Starbucks can charge for a cup of coffee, how much Rolex can charge for a watch, how much Ferrari can charge for its cars, and so forth.

Competitive Pricing

THE DEFINITION

This simply means that a company prices its products based on the prevailing pricing of similar products from competitors.

THE FORMULA AND ITS COMPONENTS

Once again, there is no formula for this.

WHERE'S THE DATA?

The data is based on market observations of competitors' pricing for similar or equivalent products.

CALCULATING IT

There is no calculation.

WHAT IT MEANS AND POTENTIAL CHALLENGES

Mass-market commodity products are the most likely candidates for this type of pricing. A visit to any gas station in the U.S. will quickly demonstrate competitive pricing at work. In Singapore, for example, petrol stations regularly discount their retail gasoline by between 7 and 10%, based on each other's pricing movements. When one drops price, the others match. As with any commodity, there are still those that can charge a price premium if their brand name is well established and positively perceived. Even though petrol is quite similar from station to station, some brands are perceived as being of higher value than others and, consequently, the manufacturers attempt to charge slightly more. In the U.S., Chevron, Shell, BP and Texaco all attempt to highlight special ingredients or additives in their gasoline, claiming improvements in engine performance and fuel efficiency if you use their brand (regularly, of course, otherwise the benefits are not sustained!).

ADVERTISING MEASURES

Advertising can be measured numerous ways depending on the media vehicle. In broadcast and Internet advertising, a few key measures are still relevant, despite the plethora of media alternatives in today's business environment. This section will discuss the following:

- Share of voice
- Advertising-to-sales ratio
- Reach
- Frequency
- Gross rating points
- Cost per gross rating point
- Click-through rates
- Profit per campaign.

Share of Uoice

THE DEFINITION

Conceptually, share of voice is the advertising equivalent to market share. It measures the percentage of its advertising expenditure a company spends on a particular product compared to the total advertising expenditure for that product in the market.

THE FORMULA AND ITS COMPONENTS

$$V_s = \frac{A}{A_t}$$

Where

V_s = your share of voice expressed in percentage terms
A = your advertising for a given product
A_t = total advertising for a given product

WHERE'S THE DATA?

Advertising totals for a particular product will be captured in the marketing plan and marketing budget. If your finance and accounting systems measure individual product investments and costs, then you may also find the advertising costs described in these reports, specifically. But it is more likely that these individual product advertising figures are "rolled-up" into an overall marketing expense line item. Market totals for advertising a given product may be found by reviewing industry trade publications, third-party research reports, business magazines with special industry sections and local business journals.

Almost every industry has a research report that you can buy from well-known research organizations such as Forrestor, Yankee, and so on. You might also find relevant stats on your niche from press releases or sales literature from organizations that have already bought the reports and are using the information in their publicity.

CALCULATING IT

Suppose $100 million is spent on ads for portable music players overall, and your company spends $5 million to promote its own player. Your share of voice would be 5%.

$$V_s = \frac{\$5,000,000}{\$100,000,000}$$

$$= 5\%$$

WHAT IT MEANS AND POTENTIAL CHALLENGES

Is share of voice really that important? Actually, yes. The reason is quite simple — advertising does have an influence on perception and a high share of voice can lead to an increased awareness which, ultimately, can lead to increased sales and market share. Sounds virtuous, doesn't it? Of course, the inverse is true as well. Additional awareness does not mean it is necessarily positive. But assuming your marketing team and advertising agency, if you have one, are good at what they do, then you should see improvement in awareness, perception, sales and share over time. Also, the number of ads you are able to run will likely have varying weights, depending on the type of audience you are trying to reach, the time of day you run the ads (if they are broadcast), or the type of publication in which you run the ads (mass market versus vertical). In essence, each of these choices is partly affected by the amount of money you wish to spend and this amount is influenced by the quality of the audience and when you try to reach them.

The magic in this number is recognizing the relationship between the amount spent and the number of ads you are able to run as a result. It is not merely about the number of ads, in other words, but the quality, as reflected in the choice of target audience, advertising medium and timing. A simple construct for understanding the potential impact of share of voice is shown in the following chart.[1]

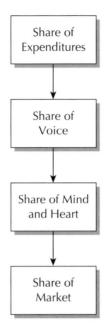

In effect, this chart suggests that your share of voice is derived from your share of advertising expenditures in the market. Furthermore, your share of voice has a direct impact on the share of mind and heart (tapping into how consumers actually feel about you and how they perceive you), which ultimately can influence your share of market. As simple as this diagram looks, do not underestimate the importance of each of the boxes it describes, because it does suggest the cause-and-effect relationship between each of the components in this chain of events.

[1] Kotler, Philip; Ang Swee Hoon; Leong Siew Meng; Tan Chin Tiong: *Marketing Management: An Asian Perspective*, p.650 ©2003 Prentice Hall.

Advertising–to–Sales Ratio

THE DEFINITION

This is a ratio that describes the effect of advertising on a company's total sales.

THE FORMULA AND ITS COMPONENTS

$$ASR = \frac{E_a}{S}$$

Where

ASR = advertising-to-sales ratio
E_a = total advertising expenditures
S = total sales

WHERE'S THE DATA?

Total advertising expenditure and total sales will both be measured in the income statement. Sometimes, income statements capture marketing expenses in one or two general categories. If so, then simply review the marketing department budget for the detail on total ad dollars spent.

CALCULATING IT

Example: Nike

Nike spent $304 million on advertising in 2003, when total sales were $10.7 billion. Its advertising-to-sales ratio was:

$$\frac{\$304,000,000}{\$10,697,000,000} = 2.8\%$$

Example: Reebok

Reebok spent approximately $106 million on advertising in 2003, when total sales were $3.485 billion. Its advertising-to-sales ratio was:

$$\frac{\$106,000,000}{\$3,485,316,000} = 3\%$$

Example: Sony

Sony spent $1.684 billion on advertising in 2003, when total sales were just over $62 billion. Its advertising-to-sales ratio was:

$$\frac{\$1,684,000,000}{\$62,031,000,000} = 2.7\%$$

Example: Samsung

Samsung spent $489,000,000 million on advertising in 2003, when total sales were just over $62 billion. Its advertising-to-sales ratio was:

$$\frac{\$489,000,000}{\$38,029,762,280} = 1.3\%$$

Example: DaimlerChrysler

DaimlerChrysler spent $2.230 billion on advertising in 2003, when total sales were nearly $172 billion. Its advertising-to-sales ratio was:

$$\frac{\$2,230,000,000}{\$171,870,000,280} = 1.3\%$$

Example: Toyota

Toyota spent $2.669 billion on advertising in 2003, when total sales were nearly $128.9 billion. Its advertising-to-sales ratio was:

$$\frac{\$2,669,000,000}{\$128,965,000,000} = 2.1\%$$

Example: Dell

Dell spent $597 million on advertising in 2003, when total sales were $35.4 billion. Its advertising-to-sales ratio was:

$$\frac{\$597,000,000}{\$35,404,000,000} = 1.7\%$$

Example: Hewlett Packard

Hewlett Packard spent $812,000,000 million on advertising in 2003, when total sales were $35.4 billion. Its advertising-to-sales ratio was:

$$\frac{\$812,000,000}{\$73,061,000,000} = 1.1\%$$

Source: AdAge Global Marketing 2004 Report

The following chart provides advertising-to-sales ratios for numerous industries and gives you a strong sense of the variation across sectors.

- Advertising-to-Sales Ratios for Selected Products, Retail Stores and Services	
Commodity or Class or Business	Average Ad Dollars as Percentage of sales
Air Courier Services	1.2%
Amusement and Recreation Services	5.2%
Apparel and Accessory Stores	3.6%
Appliance and Electronics	
Appliance Dealers	2.2%
Electronics Dealers	3.7%

(Continued)

Continued	
Commodity or Class or Business	Average Ad Dollars as Percentage of sales
Appliance and Electronics Dealers	2.7%
Auto Dealers, Gas Stations	.9%
Auto and Home Supply Stores	1.2%
Beverages	9.2%
Bicycle Dealers	2.8%
Books, Publishing & Printing	4.5%
Building Materials, Hardware, Garden (Retail)	3.2%
Cable and Other Pay TV Services	7.7%
Carpets and Rugs	0.7%
Catalog, Mail-Order Houses	6.4%
Child Day-Care Services	1.7%
Computer and Office Equipment	0.8%
Convenience Stores	0.3%
Department Stores	3.6%
Drug and Proprietary Stores	0.8%
Educational Service	6.2%
Engineering, Accounting, Research Management and Related Services	0.3%
Family Clothing Stores	2.4%
Furniture Stores	5.9%
Grocery Stores	1.0%
Hardware, Plumbing, Heating Equipment	0.6%
Hardware Stores	
Under $500,000	2.0%
$500,000–$1,000,000	2.3%
$1,000,000–$2,000,000	2.2%
Over $2,000,000	2.1%
Hobby, Toy and Game Shops	1.8%
Home Centers	
Under $2,000,000	1.5%
$2,000,000–$3,000,000	0.9%
$3,000,000–$6,000,000	0.9%
Over $6,000,000	0.9%
Home Healthcare Services	0.3%
Hospital and Medical Service Plans	0.4%
Hospitals	0.2%
Hotels and Motels	2.3%
Household Appliances	1.5%
Household Audio and Video Equipment	6.9%
Household Furniture	4.3%
Insurance Agents, Brokers and Service	1.0%
Investment Advice	1.9%
Jewelry Stores	5.1%

Continued

Commodity or Class or Business	Average Ad Dollars as Percentage of sales
Leather and Leather Products	3.9%
Legal Services	6.4%
Lumber & Other Building Materials	1.1%
Malt Beverages	8.5%
Membership Sports & Recreation Clubs	5.8%
Motions Picture Theatres	1.5%
Musical Instruments	1.5%
Office Furniture (exluding Wood)	0.8%
Office of Medical Doctors	21.3%
Ophthalmic Goods & Services	4.9%
Paints, Varnishes, Lacquers	1.2%
Perfume, Cosmetic, Toilet Preparations	7.4%
Photographic Equipment & Supplies	4.7%
Racing including Track Operations	2.8%
Radio, TV and Consumer Electronic Stores	3.2%
Real Estate Agents & Managers	4.6%
Restaurants	
Full Service, $15.00	1.9%
Full Service, $15.01–$24.99	2.1%
Full Service, $25.00	2.5%
Limited Service	0.9%
Security Brokers and Dealers	3.8%
Shoe Stores	2.5%
Skilled Nursing Care Facilities	0.5%
Sporting Goods Stores	
Full Line, <$5,000,000	1.8%
Full Line, >$5,000,000	1.9%
Specialty, <$500,000	3.5%
Specialty, $500,000–$999,999	3.3%
Specialty, >$1,000,000–$2,000,000	2.9%
Specialty,<$2,000,000–	2.8%
Television Broadcast Stations	9.3%
Tire & Inner Tubes	2.0%
Tobacco Products	4.0%
Variety Stores	0.9%
Video Tape Rental	3.5%
Women's Clothing Store	2.8%

Sources: Schonfeld & Associates, Advertising Ratios and Budgets, June 2003
North American Retail Dealers Association, Cost of Doing Business Survey Report, 2001
National Bicycle Dealers Association, The Cost of Doing Business Survey Report, 2003
National Retail Hardware Association, Cost of Doing Business Survey Report, 2002
National Restaurant Association, Restaurant Industry Operations Report, 2002
National Sporting Goods Association, Cost of Doing Business Survey Report, 2002

Source: http://www.news-record.com/advertising/advertising/ratio.html

WHAT IT MEANS AND POTENTIAL CHALLENGES

Typically, a lower advertising-to-sales ratio is better than a higher one because if you only had to spend 1 or 2% to generate a substantial revenue stream, then that implies your advertising was probably very effective in convincing your target audience. I say "probably" because we cannot *conclusively* infer that the low advertising-to-sales ratio means the ads were effective. It could be that there is a "natural" level of interest and buyer attraction to your products anyway, and that you might have achieved the same, or nearly the same, sales with little or no advertising (although that is unlikely to last for very long).

Reach

THE DEFINITION

This is the percentage of your target customers exposed, or "reached", by the media you choose to communicate your message.

A variation of this definition is the number of different consumers who view or are exposed to an advertisement, online or offline, at least once during a particular period of time.

THE FORMULA AND ITS COMPONENTS

This is not a formula. It is a measure of the audience you reach.

WHERE'S THE DATA?

This information is contained in your marketing budget, specifically in your costs. Additional detail is captured in the specific breakdowns of the media buys you make.

CALCULATING IT

For example, if your company decides to embark on a print-advertising campaign, then you will most likely do one of two things:

- You will create the ad yourself and also contact the ad department of the publications in which you want to advertise and ask for their media kit. The media kit will describe their rates (these decline the more placements you buy), and the size of the audience they reach.

OR

- You will hire an ad agency to create the ad and handle the media buy as well. The ad agency will ensure that you are reaching the right audience with the right message (if they are good).

Either way, the idea is that you choose your print advertising based on the type of audience the publications target (because they fit your customer profile) and the size of the audience.

What it Means and Potential Challenges

Let's say that you run a food stall in Singapore and you wish to attract more customers through a print-ad campaign. From experience, you know that your audience is mostly professional people between the ages of 30 and 40. So you decide to place your ad in the *Straits Times* newspaper, specifically in the business section, because it reaches the audience you want. Furthermore, you learn that the *Straits Times* reaches 52% of this audience. While this isn't bad, you want a reach of 70%, so you select one or two of the local business publications whose media kits indicate that they can add another 22% to your target audience totals. Now you are reaching 74%, which is better than you initially sought.

But you may not be successful in reaching the entire 74% simply because readers may not get to that section of the paper on some of the days you advertise, or your message does not resonate with them, or the purchasing patterns change. The point here is that you must realize that even though various media produce media kits that describe their target audiences and why those audiences are ideal to reach, there is no guarantee that the audience will be paying attention or care. So while knowing reach is important, it is not sufficiently meaningful to serve as the basis of a marketing communications campaign. You need to know more.

Frequency

THE DEFINITION

This refers to the number of advertisements a consumer is exposed to over a specified period of time.

THE FORMULA AND ITS COMPONENTS

There is no specific formula for this.

WHERE'S THE DATA?

This information comes from media kits as described in Magic Number 41.

CALCULATING IT

Calculating frequency is very straightforward and goes like this: if you buy ad space to run an ad once, then the frequency is, obviously, 1. If you buy enough ad space to run the ad twice, then your frequency is 2, and so on.

WHAT IT MEANS AND POTENTIAL CHALLENGES

The challenge to frequency is finding the right number of times to run an ad. Running an ad once is a waste of money. You need enough frequency so that the message gets through, but not so much that people tire of you. It depends on a host of factors: the size of your budget overall, the variety of marketing vehicles you are using, whether or not you are varying the message, and so forth. It is pretty hard to get it right but, from my perspective, it is critical that a campaign, if it is good, should run numerous times to have an impact. Don't abandon it just because the response from the first run was close to zero or even zero. That is simply not how marketing works and it's not how we respond to ads.

MAGIC NUM8ER 43

Gross Rating Points

THE DEFINITION

Gross rating points (GRP) describe the impact of advertising because they show how effectively the ad reached your target audience and also how frequently the ad was viewed. GRP is most often associated with television advertising.

THE FORMULA AND ITS COMPONENTS

GRP = Reach × Frequency

WHERE'S THE DATA?

The reach and frequency numbers have been described in the preceding two Magic Numbers.

CALCULATING IT

GRP is calculated as a percentage of the target market reached multiplied by the frequency of spots or exposures to that market. For example, if a marketing program includes advertising that reaches 20% of the target, and you run eight ads, then you would get the following GRP:

GRP = 20 × 8 = 160

The GRP impact is 160 GRPs.

You can plug in various numbers depending on the information contained in various media kits and determine your GRP. This will help you determine the effectiveness of your advertising decisions.

What it Means and Potential Challenges

Of course, as in the other Magic Numbers, you must be very clear about what it is you are measuring and how to interpret the results. GRP is a traditional measure of advertising, but how effective is it, really? While it is viewed as a reasonable measure of impact, this is a generous simplification. GRP measures exposures and not sales or changes in sales, so be cognizant of its true value. It is not even a perfectly precise measure of whether the ads you ran specifically created an increase in sales (although it would be reasonable to assume that if this were the only ad campaign you have been running and sales increase during or right after the campaign, then the ads were likely the reason for the increase).

Different media schedules will result in different GRP figures. If another combination of media yields a GRP of 80, then it is considered to have less "weight". Obviously, a media schedule with 250 GRPs would have more weight. But it is important to understand the frequency and reach figures to see if different GRPs are meaningful to your analysis.

Cost Per Gross Rating Point

THE DEFINITION

Cost per gross rating point (CGPRP) measures the cost of a television commercial for a specific time slot, the cost of that time slot and the gross rating points of viewers estimated for that time slot.

THE FORMULA AND ITS COMPONENTS

$$CPGRP = \frac{C_{co}}{GRP}$$

Where

C_{co} = cost per commercial time slot
GRP = gross rating points

WHERE'S THE DATA?

Please refer to Magic Numbers 41–43.

CALCULATING IT

This is a simple calculation. As we know, television advertising has become quite expensive during prime viewing time. If, for example, Singtel (a large Singapore telecom) wanted to advertise its newest hand-phone promotions on Channel News Asia's International and Singapore editions, it would be charged approximately US$1,000 for 30 seconds. Information on GRPs is not updated, but let's assume that the GRP for the 8pm to 11pm time slot is 20. We can now determine the CPGRP for this, as follows:

$$CPGRP = \frac{1,000}{20} = \$50$$

Thus, the cost per gross rating point is $50.

What it Means and Potential Challenges

CPGRP tells you the efficiency of your media cost and is effective particularly when comparing various media-buy options. An advertiser will also want to know the cost per thousand, meaning what it costs to reach every 1,000 people in the audience. But the CPGRP is a good measure to help marketing managers determine the most effective way to deploy their marketing communications expenditures. As always, marketing and media decisions are not perfect and while a particular media vehicle may describe its audience, there is no guarantee you will get precisely that audience (but it is reasonable to assume that the audience will still be quite similar to the profile the media vehicle describes). But the effectiveness of your media buy does not rest on one commercial. Repetition is important, as is message content. Furthermore, marketing managers must clearly establish objectives upfront so that measurement afterward is also effective. Finally, setting unrealistic expectations, often a disease of both marketers and CFOs (but for different reasons), will doom any commercial advertising to failure. Set achievable objectives and expectations, and chances are good that, with terrific creative execution, your message will get through.

MAG1C NUM8ER

45

Click-Through Rates

THE DEFINITION

The click-through rate is the percentage of viewers of a web advertisement who click on the banner or interstitial ad to learn more about the product or service being advertised.

THE FORMULA AND ITS COMPONENTS

$$CR = \frac{V_c}{V_t}$$

Where

CR = click-through rate
V_c = number of ad viewers who click through
V_t = total number of viewers of that ad

WHERE'S THE DATA?

The web is a marvelous tracking system and records literally every action a visitor makes to a website, where they navigated and what they clicked on. Various software packages are available, from basic website trackers for home-based websites to sophisticated packages for enterprise systems. These functions can also be outsourced to a third-party vendor, such as an ISP (Internet Service Provider), who can provide your site administrator with visitor statistics for virtually any length and point in time.

CALCULATING IT

Let's assume that your international Thai food distribution business, Hua Hin Spices, wants to attract visitors to your new line of Thai cooking spices. You decide to run a banner ad on several online gourmet food magazines. You have paid for a good placement rotation (which means your banner pops up frequently to different visitors, as opposed to only two or three times per day, randomly), so your ad is viewed by 1,000 people on its first rotation and 57 people click through to your website.

$$CR = \frac{57}{1,000} = 5.7\%$$

WHAT IT MEANS AND POTENTIAL CHALLENGES

Click-through rate is a close cousin to the "response rate" associated with direct-mail campaigns. In both cases, you are dealing with the number of people who respond to your ad out of the total number exposed to that ad. There are differences in how web ads are charged, as well. You may find sites that will charge you a flat fee for the initial ad placement and basic frequency and rotation, then also charge you a certain amount per click. Others, like Google, will simply charge you based on each click-through. The benefit to the latter is that, with luck, you have only customers who are interested in your products clicking through so, theoretically, you have a higher probability that those customers will buy. On the other hand, your competitors may be quite mean-spirited and have their receptionist click on your ad all day long, driving up your costs and sending you ultimately into bankruptcy. But let's not think about that.

MAGIC NUMBER 46

Profit Per Campaign

THE DEFINITION

This refers to the profit you make on each Internet sale, after factoring in your advertising costs.

THE FORMULA AND ITS COMPONENTS

$$PPC = (I \times CR \times C_r \times S_a \times P_m) - C_a$$

Where

PPC = profit per campaign
I = impressions
CR = click-through rate
C_r = conversion rate
S_a = average sale
P_m = profit margin
C_a = advertising cost

WHERE'S THE DATA?

See Magic Number 45 for more information.

CALCULATING IT

First, a few more terms need to be defined and discussed before we can calculate a reasonable profit per campaign.

- **Average sale** — This refers to the average sales price of each product you sell.

- **Profit margin** — As defined earlier in the book and also by sheer common sense, this is the money left over after all costs are subtracted from revenues.

- **Impressions** — This refers to the number of times your online ad is viewed (though not clicked on).

- **Advertising cost** — This is concerned with the cost of the specific online ad campaign you are assessing.

- **Profit per campaign** — This is the profit from the specific online ad campaign.

Let's continue with the Hua Hin Spices example from the previous Magic Number. We learn that Hua Hin Spices wants to buy 500,000 impressions on a website and pays $2.50 per 1,000 impressions. Furthermore, Hua Hin Spices learns from its marketing team that the industry average click-through rate is 2% (click-through rates vary widely by industry, but have generally been steadily declining over the past few years as Internet users have increasingly ignored online ads). Given the high desirability of its products, 8% of customers who click through become buyers. The average sales price of a Hua Hin Spices product is $20 and its profit margin is 35%.

Here's what we know about Hua Hin Spices:

- Advertising costs are $1,250 $\left(\$2.50 \times \dfrac{500,000}{1,000}\right)$

- 10,000 people will visit its site ($500,000 \times 2\%$)

- 800 of these people will buy products ($10,000 \times 8\%$)

- $16,000 in revenues will be produced ($800 \times \$20$ per sale)

- $5,600 in profits will result ($\$16,000 \times 35\%$).

Now we can measure the profitability of this specific campaign.

$PPC = (I \times CR \times C_r \times S_a \times P_m) - C_a$

$PPC = (500,000 \times .02 \times .08 \times 20 \times .35) - \$1,250 = \$4,350$

What it Means and Potential Challenges

Profit per campaign is quite obviously a tool to measure the profitability of a specific online ad campaign. It is dependent on gathering the right data (specifics on click-through rates for your industry, current costs for banner ads, advertising fee policies of chosen sites and the appeal of your products to an online audience). These kinds of metrics are fairly easy to collect in general and the formula is drop-dead simple, making it a convenient tool to measure success. In combination with other advertising metrics and profitability measures, you should have a fair amount of ammunition to use against the finance department if it complains that marketing doesn't measure its efforts.

RETAIL MARKETING MEASURES

Since a great deal of consumer business is conducted at the retail-store level, it is important to understand how retailers measure success. There are several measures designed to address information needs both at corporate headquarters and store levels.

Corporate-level measures enable the main accounting, finance and strategic marketing functions to understand performance system-wide. The main corporate-level measures are:

- Turnover

- Gross margin return on inventory investment

- Sales per square foot

- Sales/profit per employee.

Store-level measures are:

- Average transaction size

- Average items

- Conversion rate.

There are many ways to interpret and use the data resulting from using these measures that assist the retailer in developing a merchandise mix and marketing plan that maximizes its attractiveness to consumers. Each of these measures helps retailers understand an important area of their business and each reveals insights about consumers, merchandise and even the in-store sales performance of its employees.

MAG1C NUM8ER

47

Turnover

THE DEFINITION

Turnover measures how quickly total inventory is produced and sold, usually over the course of a year.

THE FORMULA AND ITS COMPONENTS

$$\text{Turnover} = \frac{S}{I_a}$$

Where

S = sales
I_a = average inventory

Note: average inventory is usually calculated as the sum of each month's Beginning of Month inventory figures (12 in all) plus the last End of Month inventory amount, then divided by 13.

WHERE'S THE DATA?

Data is most likely tracked at the warehouse level and is also found in the balance sheet under "current assets".

CALCULATING IT

Suppose your company has a chain of 20 retail outlets and your sales last year were $40 million. Your average inventory each month was $4 million. Your turnover, then, equals 10, as follows:

$$\text{Turnover} = \frac{\$40,000,000}{\$4,000,000}$$

$$= 10$$

What it Means and Potential Challenges

For retail accounts, a turnover of 10 is typically quite good. In effect, turnover is measuring the velocity of inventory change and, since inventory represents money (invested) sitting in a warehouse, the sooner it is sold, then the sooner the investment earns returns. So a high inventory turnover is a good sign. Particularly with perishables, or non-durable goods, a high turnover is paramount since spoilage is a very real risk. However, durable goods are also important to turn over quickly since they generate revenues that can then be put to use in newer inventory and for other productive purposes. Turnover is a key measure of retail productivity.

Gross Margin Return on Inventory Investment

THE DEFINITION

Gross margin return on inventory investment (GMROII) measures how successfully a retailer has invested its money used for inventory.

THE FORMULA AND ITS COMPONENTS

The formula is straightforward:

$$GMROII = \frac{GM}{C_{ai}}$$

Where

GMROII = gross margin return on inventory investment
GM $\quad$ = gross margin (dollars)
C_{ai} $\quad$ = average inventory costs

WHERE'S THE DATA?

Typically, this information is in the accounting and finance statements, usually under the consolidated statement of earnings.

CALCULATING IT

Let's assume that a sporting goods retailer chain is earning gross margins of $3 million. Average inventory at cost is $1,000,000. Therefore, the GMROII is $3, calculated as follows:

$$\text{GMROII} = \frac{\$3,000,000}{\$1,000,000}$$

$$= \$3$$

WHAT IT MEANS AND POTENTIAL CHALLENGES

Essentially, it is a measure of your inventory's productivity as it helps describe the relationship between key retail performance measures: total sales, the gross profit margin earned on sales, and the number of dollars invested in inventory. In this example, $1 of investment earned $3 in return. Another way to explain this is that GMROII tells you how much you've earned back on your original inventory investment during one year.

Sales Per Square Foot

THE DEFINITION

This measure determines how productive a retailer is with the use of retail space for merchandising to generate and maximize sales.

THE FORMULA AND ITS COMPONENTS

$$SPSF = \frac{S}{S_a}$$

Where

SPSF = sales per square foot
S   = total sales
S_a = selling area in square feet

WHERE'S THE DATA?

See Magic Number 48. Also, many retailers have requirements for frequent field reporting from each retail location. This information is fed into the main company reporting statements. These can be weekly or monthly. Information on each store's square footage should be available in the detailed notes of the company's tangible assets. As the sales are reported, they can then be aggregated company wide to determine the correct amount.

CALCULATING IT

Suppose that our sporting goods retailer has total sales of $20 million and a total selling area across all stores of 100,000 square feet. The sales per square foot is $200, calculated as follows:

$$SPSF = \frac{\$20,000,000}{\$100,000}$$

$$= \$200$$

WHAT IT MEANS AND POTENTIAL CHALLENGES

It is important to note that selling area refers to the areas of the store devoted to actual selling space, as opposed to window displays (to which consumers have no access), dressing rooms (where no merchandise is displayed for sale) and similar non-selling floor space. Also, vacant space costs money (much like an empty airline seat costs money), so the productive use of existing space is critical to successful sales. At its most fundamental level, this measures the productivity of the space available for selling.

Sales/Profit Per Employee

THE DEFINITION

This is a measure of financial performance on an individual-employee basis.

THE CALCULATION AND ITS COMPONENTS

$$SPPE = \frac{S \text{ or } P}{E}$$

Where

SPPE = sales/profit per employee
S   = sales
P   = profits
E   = total number of full-time employees

WHERE'S THE DATA?

The sales and profit data comes from the company's financial statements, specifically from the income statement. The employee information is most likely in the human resource files. This data refers only to full-time employees.

CALCULATING IT

Let's continue with the sporting goods company example from Magic Numbers 48 and 49. This company has 400 full-time employees. Its sales per employee is therefore $50,000, calculated as follows:

$$SPPE = \frac{\$20,00,000}{400}$$

$$= \$50,000$$

WHAT IT MEANS AND POTENTIAL CHALLENGES

Sales/profit per employee is a critical measure of productivity. It helps a retailer gauge, in effect, the amount generated (either revenues or profits) per employee. A lower figure is an indication that either the company is over-staffed or under-productive with its employees and that, therefore, ways must be found to improve this. Training might prove to be a worthwhile investment, for example; or perhaps new point-of-sale technology that makes operations and consumer tracking more efficient, allowing employees to take better care of customers.

Average Transaction Size

THE DEFINITION

This measures the average value of each transaction/sale.

THE FORMULA AND ITS COMPONENTS

$$T_a = \frac{S}{T}$$

Where

T_a = average transaction size
S = total value of sales
T = total number of transactions

WHERE'S THE DATA?

This data is captured every day. Well-run retailers do their end-of-day totals to review the day's performance and to close the books for that day so that the next day can be measured anew. Point-of-purchase systems will usually measure each transaction individually, by item and selling price. Even manual systems record each sale, so either way the information should be captured at the store level by each store manager.

CALCULATING IT

Assuming our sporting goods retailer generates $1 million in sales from each store annually, and the total number of transactions is

50,000, then the average transaction size is $20 per transaction per store.

$$T_a = \frac{\$1,000,000}{50,000}$$

$$= \$20$$

What it Means and Potential Challenges

Retailers want to know how much the average customer spends per transaction so that they can develop strategies and programs to improve the per-transaction sales value. It is really a matter of persuading customers who are already committed to buying, to buy more. Ideally, retailers want to see the average transaction size increase year over year because this is a measure of their productivity and success at selling products. Furthermore, the transaction size can be an indicator of the types of items that sell well and those that do not. By understanding this, retailers can also develop a plan that improves their merchandise mix (the selection of items available for sale in the store).

Average Items Per Transaction

THE DEFINITION

This measures the average number of items bought per customer.

THE FORMULA AND ITS COMPONENTS

$$S_{avg} = \frac{S}{T}$$

Where

S_{avg} = average number of items sold per transaction
S = total number of items sold
T = total number of transactions

WHERE'S THE DATA?

See the previous Magic Number.

CALCULATING IT

Our sporting goods retailer has quite an in-store inventory and sold 150,000 items in one year. The average number of items per transaction is three, as calculated below:

$$S_{avg} = \frac{150,000}{50,000}$$

$$= 3$$

WHAT IT MEANS AND POTENTIAL CHALLENGES

Since this measures the average number of items each customer buys, it helps a retailer understand the buying behavior of its customer base. If this number increases over time, it can be interpreted in a few ways. It may tell a retailer that its merchandise mix is attractive and customers like to buy items related to a specific sport or category. It could also indicate that customers like variety. A clever retailer will want to understand the mix of items on each transaction to see if there are interesting patterns or trends to be exploited. It may also correlate to a specific promotions or advertising campaign that ran simultaneously with an increase in the number of items sold per transaction.

53 Retailer's Margin Percentage

THE DEFINITION

This is the profit margin that retailers realize after purchasing from the wholesaler and then selling to the consumer. It is a measure of how much money the retailer makes.

THE FORMULA AND ITS COMPONENTS

$$RMP = \frac{(S_p - P_p)}{S_p}$$

Where

RMP = retailer's margin in percentage terms
S_p = selling price to consumers
P_p = purchase price from wholesalers

WHERE'S THE DATA?

The selling price to consumers is not always the target retail price set by manufacturers because the target price does not factor in slotting fees, co-op marketing, promotional allowances and other similar marketing programs. These types of fees are usually set at the corporate level and each retail outlet is expected to adhere to company standards. However, retailers will have their own set of pricing and profit guidelines for each product they sell, often down to the individual store level (since goals may vary slightly from market to market, even if the store is part of a chain). In some cases, the corporate strategy may include a tacit understanding that each store manager has limited freedom to adjust corporate requirements based on the prevailing market situation in a given area. The wholesale sales price can be found on invoices, purchase orders and accounting reports.

CALCULATING IT

Suppose a retailer is selling a toiletry item at a retail price of $5 and the price paid to the wholesaler was $2.50. Calculating the retailer's margin percentage is an easy exercise:

$$RMP = \frac{(\$5 - \$2.50)}{\$5}$$
$$= 50\%$$

WHAT IT MEANS AND POTENTIAL CHALLENGES

The retailer's margin percentage is a key positioning component. It reflects the retailer's strategy in attracting the target audience. If a retailer selects a premium price position, it is most likely trying to achieve higher profits. However, higher margins are usually not associated with high volume. Conversely, lower margins may signal a more aggressive position to grow demand, but margins are adversely affected and unless volumes are consistently high, then low-price retailers can often face negative returns, especially during slower selling cycles. There are fairly sophisticated strategic approaches to margins that include whether a retailer focuses on store brands rather than national or global brands. Increasing evidence indicates that store brands allow a retailer to increase its margins, even accounting for the in-house production and manufacturing costs, over non-store, national brands. For companies like WalMart, this can be a very effective approach, especially if they do not get the margin concessions they expect from large international brands. A smaller, less well-known retailer may depend on non-store brands simply because it does not have the financial wherewithal to develop its own product line. Alternatively, a mixed strategy may be a successful approach for certain retailers. Again, WalMart comes to mind, as does Carrefour from France. While we have examined a basic approach to determining retailer's margin percentages, there are many variables that can directly influence the final retail margin percentage.

DIRECT MARKETING MEASURES

Direct marketing is a powerful tool to reach consumers, especially when done properly. By "when done properly", I am referring to direct marketing that clearly has a specific offer and benefit. Spam (either electronic or the traditional junk mail) is increasingly the cause of irritation and anger among consumers. Therefore, marketers must use direct marketing in a way that invites consumer loyalty, not repels it. I cannot provide you with guidelines for this except to say you know what it is like when you are inundated with unwanted, even offensive, messages. I suggest you take the proverbial high road and ensure you craft direct-marketing messages that are thoughtful and compelling rather than mindless. Will every consumer respond? No. But the measures in the following section will assist marketers in assessing the attractiveness and success of their direct-marketing efforts.

Response Rate

MAGIC NUM8ER 54

THE DEFINITION

The response rate refers to the ratio of people who respond to an offer relative to the number of people who receive the offer.

THE FORMULA AND ITS COMPONENTS

$$R_r = \frac{P_r}{P_e}$$

Where

R_r = response rate
P_r = number of people who respond to your ad
P_e = number of people exposed to your ad

WHERE'S THE DATA?

The numbers come from your own statistics based on your direct-marketing objectives. If your goal is to mail to 10,000 people in your target audience, then those names come from your own database, a third-party database, or a combination of these two. Typically, as described elsewhere in this book, if your goal is a higher response rate, then it is recommended you use a reputable list of either customers who have bought from you before or a list of customers who appear to fit your profile. A random mailing to the general population (believe it or not, some businesses have done this) is both sloppy and provides a low response. A proven in-house list of customers is best since they are already familiar with your company and have bought from you before. A third-party list can be quite good, if you understand your target audience clearly and if the third-party vendor has a reputation for providing high-quality names.

CALCULATING IT

If your company targets 10,000 people in its direct mailing and receives 800 responses, then your response rate is:

$$R_r = \frac{800}{10,000}$$

$$= 8\%$$

WHAT IT MEANS AND POTENTIAL CHALLENGES

The response rate is a basic measure that can indicate the percentage of people who find your offer attractive. Typically, if they respond, this can lead to purchase, but it is not a guarantee. A response may also be a request for additional information. This depends on the wording in your offer. If it is clear to recipients of the direct-mail effort that they will get something by responding (such as a price discount on a favorite product, or a free gift with purchase), then the chances of converting them to actual buyers increases significantly. However, if the offer is somewhat vague, such as describing a "hot new feature" but no other benefit, it is likely that there will be fewer who actually buy the product. The reason for this is that direct-mail marketing has proven, over the years, to be most successful when it is offering a tangible benefit that can be easily gained, as opposed to general awareness advertising, which tends to be better suited for broadcast. Direct mail also works well for shorter-term promotions, in which you are trying encourage immediate demand. Classic marketing theory suggests that if you can convince customers to buy your product, then you have a better chance of making them loyal customers. Of course, that is dependent on your commitment to quality, service and products that are relevant. That is not as easy as it sounds.

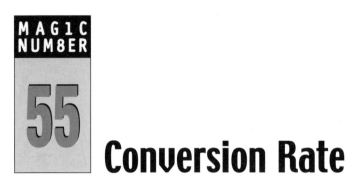

MAGIC NUM8ER

55

Conversion Rate

THE DEFINITION

Conversion rate is described as the percentage of prospective customers (to an offer) or visitors (to a website) who both respond and buy a company's products and services.

THE FORMULA AND ITS COMPONENTS

$$C_r = \frac{P_b}{P_r}$$

Where

C_r = conversion rate
P_b = number of people who both respond and buy
P_r = number of people who respond to your ad

WHERE'S THE DATA?

See the previous Magic Number. Also, note that the data for the number of people who actually buy will be captured in your financial statements on a regular basis (daily if online, or weekly/monthly for other retailers). Typically, to know whether those who bought are from the direct-mail campaign, companies can put a reference code in the mailing that consumers must mention to receive the special offer. Similar types of reference tags can be used to track response to specific campaigns.

CALCULATING IT

Continuing with the numbers from the example given in Magic Number 54, if 75 people out of the 800 who respond buy a product, then the conversion rate is 9.4%.

$$C_r = \frac{75}{800} = 9.4\%$$

WHAT IT MEANS AND POTENTIAL CHALLENGES

Without question, companies should strive for a high conversion rate because this is an indication that your offer was attractive enough to not just warrant a response, but to induce the responder to buy. Achieving a high conversion rate depends on many variables, including the relevance and appeal of the offer to the target customer, how easily accessible the offer is, the visual design, appropriate price, and how it compares to competing offers. With this list of qualifiers, it does appear to be a daunting task to develop a successful campaign. But that is the beauty of marketing — it is part art and part science.

MAG1C NUM8ER

56

Direct-Mail Revenue Goals

THE DEFINITION

This is an approach to measuring the effectiveness of your direct-mail advertising through setting a revenue target, with which you can then determine the number of direct-mail pieces that need to be sent to achieve that target.

THE FORMULA AND ITS COMPONENTS

$$DM = \frac{R_t}{S_a \times R_r \times C_r}$$

Where

DM = number of direct-mail pieces
R_t = revenue target
S_a = average sale
R_r = response rate
C_r = conversion rate

WHERE'S THE DATA?

These statistics should be available in your marketing budget and from any customer data that you have. Elsewhere I refer to the importance of gathering the latest statistics for direct marketing in your particular industry and target customer base. This research should provide you with a good sense of response and conversion rates so that you can then compare these to those of other companies in your business. Revenue targets for a direct-marketing campaign should be an element of the overall revenue targets for the organization.

CALCULATING IT

In the following example, Tammi's Tantalizing Taste Treats is a small confectionary store just off Orchard Avenue in Singapore (the main shopping district of the city). Tammi is keenly interested in increasing her revenue by $40,000, and the customer list she wants to acquire is filled with people who love sweets, but she wants to know how many direct-mail pieces she needs to send to achieve her revenue target. She knows that out of 200 customers who visit her store each day, 150 buy confectionary. This gives her a conversion rate of 75%. Those who buy spend an average of $30. Tammi has done her homework on her industry and knows that the average response rate is 3% for direct-mail campaigns promoting confectionary.

$$DM = \frac{\$40,000}{\$30 \times .03 \times .75}$$

$$= 59,259 \text{ pieces}$$

If Tammi is clever, she might be able to craft a message that is so tantalizing that it increases the response rate to 5%. This improvement would decrease the number of mailing pieces she needs to send to 35,555 (as shown below), which would also reduce the amount of money she would have to spend on printing and postage.

$$DM = \frac{\$40,000}{\$30 \times .03 \times .75}$$

$$= 59,259 \text{ pieces}$$

WHAT IT MEANS AND POTENTIAL CHALLENGES

The benefit to this analysis is that it enables the marketing manager to more carefully determine costs upfront, although this is only an estimate since the campaign has yet to occur. Another dimension to this is that Tammi will gain 1,333 new customers (59,259 × .03 × .75) who could become regular if she treats them well. So while this particular campaign may produce the $40,000 revenue increase she is seeking, it also has the potential to make some of these customers more loyal over the long term, adding to her customer base and creating, in effect, an ongoing customer revenue stream.

Direct-Mail Profit Goals

The Definition

This refers to setting a target profitability level to determine the number of direct-mail pieces that need to be sent to achieve your goal.

The Formula and its Components

The formula is nearly identical to that for direct-mail revenue goals, except that the denominator includes the target profit percentage, as follows:

$$DM = \frac{R_t}{S_a \times P \times R_r \times C_r}$$

Where

P = profit goal in percentage terms

Where's the Data?

Refer to Magic Number 56.

Calculating It

To continue with the example of Tammi's Tantalizing Taste Treats from the previous Magic Number, let's assume that her target profit margin is 30%. This factor is added to the formula as follows:

$$DM = \frac{\$40,000}{\$30 \times .30 \times .03 \times .75}$$

$$= 197,531$$

No one could ever accuse Tammi of being timid. She believes her product is superior and wants high margins to reflect premium value. The impact of this on the cost of her mailing campaign is significant, however. If, as with the previous Magic Number, Tammi were to create an offer that might yield a 5% response, then she would need to mail "only" 118,519 pieces to achieve the same profit target.

$$DM = \frac{\$40,000}{\$30 \times .30 \times .05 \times .75}$$

$$= 118,519$$

What it Means and Potential Challenges

The benefits and risks are similar to those with direct-mail revenue goals. Whether or not a particular profit goal is feasible in your business will be determined by a profitability analysis for your industry and a keen knowledge of the industry's dynamics.

MAGIC NUM8ER

58 Direct–Mail Gross Profit

THE DEFINITION

This calculation tells you whether your direct-mail campaign produces a positive gross profit.

THE FORMULA AND ITS COMPONENTS

$$P_g = DM \times P \times S_a \times R_r \times C_r$$

Where

P_g = gross profit
P = profit goal in percentage terms
DM = number of direct-marketing pieces
S_a = average sale
R_r = response rate
C_r = conversion rate

WHERE'S THE DATA?

Once again, as in the previous two Magic Numbers, the data comes from a combination of internal goals and external sources.

CALCULATING IT

Let's plug in the numbers from the previous two Magic Numbers, in which we used the example of Tammi's Tantalizing Tasty Treats.

$$P_g = 59,259 \times .30 \times \$30 \times .03 \times .75$$
$$= \$12,000$$

What it Means and Potential Challenges

Tammi's gross profit looks quite good and, at this stage, it would indicate that she should go forward with the campaign. However, it would be smart for Tammi and her team to check the net profit to ensure that this is the right move.

MAGIC NUM8ER

59

Direct–Mail Net Profit

The Definition

Calculating this helps you determine if your direct-mail campaign produces a positive net profit.

The Formula and its Components

This is virtually identical to the formula for direct-mail gross profit, with one new component included:

$$P_g = DM \times P \times S_a \times R_r \times C_r - C_{dm}$$

Where

C_{dm} = cost of the direct-mail campaign

Where's the Data?

See previous Magic Numbers on direct marketing in Part One of this book.

Calculating It

Using the same numbers as before, we now include the cost of the direct-mail campaign. In this case, Tammi outsourced the design and printing work, which cost her $8,000.

$$P_g = 59,259 \times .30 \times \$30 \times .03 \times .75 - \$8,000$$
$$= \$4,000$$

What it Means and Potential Challenges

Tammi can relax a little, knowing that her campaign estimates indicate she will produce a net profit. The point to this particular sequence is to demonstrate the various levels of analysis needed to determine the efficacy of a direct-marketing campaign. Numerous factors are within the direct control of any company: goals, size of mailing list, content of offer and industry metrics. The harder area to control is consumer behavior. There is no guarantee that, despite your analytical rigor and the elegance of your business plan, your customers will respond as you would like. But knowing this can help you develop a certain creativity AND patience in your marketing efforts. Doing so will enable you to learn those activities that work best for you, as well as those that missed the mark.

Direct-Mail ROI

THE DEFINITION

This is the return on your direct-mail investment.

THE FORMULA AND ITS COMPONENTS

$$ROI = \frac{((DM \times R_r \times C_r \times S_a) - C)}{C}$$

Where

DM = total number of direct-marketing pieces sent
R_r = response rate
C_r = conversion rate of people who bought something
S_a = average sales per purchase
C   = total cost of direct-mail campaign

WHERE'S THE DATA?

As with the other Magic Numbers concerned with direct marketing, the data for understanding ROI depends on the direct-mail list you use (in-house, third-party, random) and how many pieces you mail. Also, the response and conversion rates depend on the industry and the offer. In both cases, these rates will vary, so know your benchmark metrics and your objectives in advance so that it is easier to measure success once the campaign is under way.

CALCULATING IT

Let's assume that the tournament directors of the Australian Open tennis tournament (one of four tennis Grand Slam events, in case you don't follow tennis) want to measure the ROI for a very special direct-mail campaign they are sending to people who love tennis. The campaign offers center-court seats for the finals to the first person to guess correctly the number of tennis balls there are in an empty swimming pool shown on the cover of the direct-mail piece. The goals of the campaign are twofold: to build pre-tournament excitement that will please their sponsors, and to generate more interest in Australian tourism. The direct-mail piece has a tournament website address that will, with luck, encourage recipients to visit the site and the new Australian Open Logo apparel shop online.

The tournament promotions director decides to send this mailing to 250,000 tennis fans around the world, at a total cost of $200,000. The organizers' research has shown that specialty direct-mail campaigns marketing super-luxury goods such as this tend to get a very high response rate of 25%. Of the 250,000 people targeted, they anticipate that 62,500 will respond and that many more will visit the website and buy merchandise even though they won't attend the tournament. They expect 10% of the respondents, 6,250 people, to convert to sales at the tournament's online website. Furthermore, based on previous years' experience, the average amount spent per customer is $200. The calculation is thus as follows:

$$\text{ROI} = \frac{((250{,}000 \times .25 \times .10 \times \$200) - \$200{,}000)}{\$200{,}000}$$

$$= 525\%$$

This is a substantial return on investment!

WHAT IT MEANS AND POTENTIAL CHALLENGES

As with any ROI calculation, direct-mail ROI will give you an indication of the success of a particular investment. In this instance, we were examining an expected mailing, response and conversion. The final test would be to revisit this ROI after the event with actual numbers. But from these preliminary forecasts, it is apparent that this is an attractive marketing opportunity.

MARKET RESEARCH MEASURE

This book covers key marketing strategy and marketing management measures and frameworks. Market research is an important and separate field of study around which an entire industry has grown and specific techniques and methodologies have been developed that are beyond the scope of this book. However, marketers often have to consider whether to invest in market research to further their understanding of the marketplace. U.S. and European companies, in particular, more regularly devote a portion of their total marketing budget to market research. This is less so at Asian companies, although there is a growing emphasis on market research throughout the Asia Pacific region.

To this end, a useful guide is Magic Number 61 on the following pages. Like any Magic Number, this should be used along with a healthy amount of judgment and input from colleagues and any available industry information or standards since, despite its formulaic design, is still only a guide.

61 Market–Research Budget

THE DEFINITION

The market-research budget (MRB) reflects the investment the company wishes to make to understand a market.

THE FORMULA AND ITS COMPONENTS

$B = C \times R \times F$

Where

B = budget
C = is the cost associated with making an error or a
    bad judgment

Companies do make bad choices and they can be expensive. "C" here is the negative financial impact resulting from choosing the incorrect target market, the wrong product design, poor pricing decisions, a poorly executed marketing campaign...

R = the percentage reduction in the chances of making an error that
    comes from wise investment in market research

Companies often have the capability to make sound, informed decisions based on knowledge of the market. This knowledge is acquired through thoughtful market research.

F = a pre-set, internal guideline for establishing a reasonable[1]
    marketing research budget.

F decreases the maximum amount (the product of C × R) to a more feasible[2] level.

WHERE'S THE DATA?

The budget number is based on in-house forecasts from your marketing, sales and product teams. Determining the percentage reduction in the chances of making a mistake is truly a guesstimate. A marketing manager should ask, "If I plan thoughtful research, how much do I think that this will reduce my chances of making a bad decision?" In other words, almost any investment a company makes in its business is a cost for a period of time until it produces results that, if all goes well, off-set the original investment and also provide a profit. Market research, by itself, is not a profit or revenue center (generally), but it can have a direct impact on profits since it often informs the decisions for new products. If the research is of high quality, reliable and answers specific questions you have about the customers and market needs, then it can reduce some of the investment cost in product development, since you would not be engaging in as much risky trial-and-error prototyping.

CALCULATING IT

Let's assume that Kao, the Japanese manufacturer of soaps, cosmetics and chemical products (among others), has a marketing manager who is interested in determining the market's interest in a new detergent. He decides to conduct market research, but the general manager (GM) wants to know how much this research will cost before agreeing to it. Since it is a new product competing in an existing category, educating the consumer is not as necessary as it might be for, say, a new technology. The GM asks her marketing manager a few questions:

- How large are the forecast revenues?

- What is the expected gross profit?

- How much would gross profits be affected if there were an error in its final formulation?

The marketing manager offers the following plan:

- $90 million in forecast revenue

- $10 million in expected gross profits

- $8.5 million reduction in gross profits if an error is made

- 15% reduction in the chances of making an error if proper market research is conducted.

The marketing manager is quite excited, and tells the GM that a sizable research budget is needed, based on this calculation:

$$B = \$10,000,000 \times .15$$
$$= \$1,500,000$$

No wonder he is so excited. A $1.5 million market research budget would be the envy of many marketing departments. Alas, our young marketing manager has neglected an important factor: knowing what is feasible. The GM tells him that Kao generally has a feasibility percentage of around 7.5% applied to projects. In light of this, the marketing manager is obliged to recalculate his market-research estimate thus:

$$B = \$10,000,000 \times .15 \times .075$$
$$= \$112,500$$

While the marketing manager is somewhat deflated by this substantially reduced amount, from the GM's perspective a $112,500 investment to generate $90 million in revenues and $10 million in expected gross profits is quite appealing.

WHAT IT MEANS AND POTENTIAL CHALLENGES

When contemplating a marketing research effort, it pays to consider the potential repercussions of proceeding with a project in the absence of this research. Consider the penalty for a wrong decision, such as merely guessing about the target market. In the event that this is the wrong decision, in our example the gross profit would be reduced by $8.5 million. Thus, it is important to estimate the potential reduction in gross profit that would come from not investing in quality research.

Often, marketing people focus on generating revenues and gross profits, to the exclusion of the cost side of the business. Our marketing manager in this example was quite happy to seek, and possibly spend, $1.5 million as he no doubt saw $90 million in revenues and $10 million in gross profit as being attractive. The counter-argument is that he would have invested a substantial sum to learn information that could be discovered less expensively, as the GM counseled. The important point is to determine how much your chances of error in going to market are reduced by conducting research that is relevant to your understanding of the market.

Marketing managers need to determine a reasonable, *feasible* market-research budget that does not merely lead to break-even, but facilitates profitability. In the example above, our marketing manager could have spent more than 10 times as much to do the market research. But investing the maximum with the prospect of uncertain returns is risky. Furthermore, a financial manager would ask the simple question, "What are the opportunity costs associated with this project?" In other words, could the company earn more from the same investment if deployed differently (i.e. not in research, but in hiring a sales person, or enhancing the product's features, or spending more on retail promotions with existing accounts)? Thus, a reasonable rule of thumb is to discount the maximum budget, as we did here. In this case, the company could opt for the following courses of action:

- Invest the full $1.5 million in the market-research project and either run the risk that the money is spent on the wrong market, with the attendant loss of $8.5 million of gross profit, or learn that the right market was chosen, yielding the $90 million in revenue and $10 million in gross profit (less the $1.5 million entailed in the market-research project).

- Invest $112,500 and have similar outcomes to the above, but at lower cost.

- Invest either amount in its entirety on some other project with a more attractive opportunity cost.

- Not invest the money at all and forgo the opportunity to launch the new product

There are a few more combinations of investments that could be considered, but this certainly provides a reasonable range of options.

As you can see, even with this "formula", there is still some guesswork involved. How do companies determine the potential reduction in gross profits if they make a wrong decision? How should the feasible market-research percentage be determined? What is the best way to determine the reduction in error if proper research is conducted? The list goes on. As you have read in this book, most of the Magic Numbers for Consumer Marketing have challenges associated with them. This does not make them any less useful, but it does mean they are not infallible. There is no substitute for sound judgment as a complement to model-driven analysis.

[1,2] The terms "reasonable" and "feasible" are obviously a bit vague and border on the unhelpful. This is further complicated by the use of marketing research by companies in different regions of the world. U.S. and European companies, particularly large Fortune 500-type firms, often have sizable market-research budgets. These budgets support the activities of professional market-research teams, both internal and third-party, devoted to learning about customers, competitors, trends and economic issues, in the pursuit of knowledge that can help the companies make more-informed product decisions. Even SME (small to mid-size enterprises) in these regions will devote a portion of their marketing budget to research activities. The use of marketing research is less consistently employed in many Asian firms and is often considered a luxury. Given these regional differences, it becomes apparent that defining "reasonable" and "feasible" is quite challenging. Certainly, any company considering marketing research must first ask a few basic questions:

- Why do we want to conduct research in the first place?
- What are we trying to learn?
- What will we do with the information we gather?
- What research methodology should we employ (probability, non-probability, surveys, conjoint, data reduction….the list of market research tools and methods is extensive)?
- How will we analyze the data?
- How will we store and access the data?

Answering these questions is a good start, and there are more resources that the energetic marketer can review. Several are listed in the appendix at the end of this book.

Thus, assuming you decide marketing research is important to your company and you have answered the questions above (among others), then what is reasonable and feasible becomes a matter of what you think your business can afford. If the amount your company can afford (or that you are willing to devote) is still quite small, then you may find that the research you conduct will not be statistically valid or of added value. Of course, now you may ask, "What is 'quite small'?" This is a perfectly reasonable question, to which I do not have an answer that would apply universally to all companies. Instead, you will have to spend the time determining what is the minimum you can spend and still learn something useful. I apologize to those who want more precision. Unfortunately, not everything in the daily practice of business is always neatly prescribed. As already mentioned, you will regularly have to make decisions based on incomplete information.

Using the Magic Numbers in a Marketing Plan

As we have discovered, each of the Magic Numbers for Consumer Marketing can help marketers organize and evaluate the success of their marketing efforts. There is increasing emphasis today on measuring the results of most business activities, and marketing, in particular, is regularly targeted within organizations as an area that needs to improve its analysis of how its role contributes to the success of the firm. I say these words with some trepidation because there are still areas of business that defy even the keenest of formulas and measures. And, as stated throughout this book, numbers have yet to be devised that predict consumer behavior perfectly and *accurately*.

There is no doubt that marketers need to be smarter in how they measure the performance of their organizations and the programs they develop and implement. But I caution that a stronger emphasis on measuring marketing, while undoubtedly productive and useful, will not yield the information that many business leaders seek. Because the pressure to measure risks is a journey without end, it has the potential to create artificial (and possibly unreasonable) expectations which could actually harm the impact marketing can have in developing a company's relationships with its customers and the market. The underlying reason for this is the inherent subjectivity of the buyer-seller relationship itself. Despite the best information and convincing communications, consumers will still make decisions that are heavily influenced by emotion, wrestling reason to the floor and reducing the quantitative analysis to little more than a quaint exercise in math. For these numbers to truly have magic, marketers need to artfully blend use of the Magic Numbers for Consumer Marketing with compelling arguments for the human side of transacting business. This, too, is a journey without end. In fact, the magic of marketing is in recognizing that it is a process that unfolds much as the chapters in a book lead you to the next step in the story. Each marketing chapter is written just ahead of when it is read, containing some idea of the general direction of the plot, but lacking in a precise ending because businesses are theoretically designed to live well beyond the lifespan of most people. So a marketer's, indeed any manager's, obligation is to keep writing the business story, knowing that the destination won't be reached for quite a while and that the pathways will be built and expanded by each succeeding generation of leaders.

With this in mind, I include below a framework for a marketing plan that illustrates where, at each stage of the plan, a marketer would be most likely to use each of the Magic Numbers set out in this book. Keep in mind that including these measures does not address every information need required in a marketing plan. There are many facets of marketing that I have left out because this is a book about measuring marketing and not about marketing strategy or management. These guidelines are just the starting point.

Marketing Plan: Outline and Contents

Marketing plans are a key tool to describe the strategies and tactics you wish to undertake in support of developing your business. The detail in marketing plans varies by company and industry, but the absence of a plan might suggest a disregard for common sense. While I was at Nike, three-page action plans were the norm, while at Transamerica, a comprehensive strategic analysis of several dozen pages was expected. Which one was correct? Each was right for that company, based on its culture and its operating behavior.

Any marketing plan should also include information regarding a number of other areas crucial to the company's operations. These are set out below in each of the sections and linked to the appropriate Magic Numbers outlined in this book. The fundamental aspects of the plan will usually include the following:

Executive Summary

This is a brief (usually only one or two pages) overview of the key ideas described in the body of the marketing plan. Typically, this includes the overall strategy, key goals and main recommendations, providing management with a concise summary of the main points of the plan.

Table of Contents

Situation Analysis & Review

This section answers the question: where are we now? This includes describing the company's current financial performance, product reviews and competitive standing. A SWOT analysis (strengths, weaknesses, opportunities, threats) is developed which outlines key variables that can influence business performance.

Recommended Magic Numbers to Assess the Current Market

- **Market Size**

- **Market Growth**

- **Market Share**

- **Market Penetration**

- **Market-Share Index**

Particular attention should be paid to the firm's strengths and weaknesses to enable managers to determine more effectively the challenges to be overcome and the key assets that can be exploited to create value and advantage. In addition, the firm must assess market threats to defend itself against and the opportunities to pursue that have yet to be fully realized. Determining the value of your brand helps you more fully understand the influences on this valuable asset.

Recommended Magic Numbers to Evaluate Value

- **Brand-Value Frameworks**

- **Brand Equity**

- **Brand-Name Premium**

Of course, as we have discovered, brands are more than a financial measure or model. They comprise people with unique talents organized to harness the maximum potential of the firm. Understanding the strengths of your people will help you align resources more effectively as marketing programs and responsibilities are assigned.

Recommended Magic Number to Review Your Organization

- **Brand-Culture Framework**

Another dimension is measuring whether and how well consumers are aware of your company and/or its brands. Having this information helps you develop communications messages that more accurately reflect the market's understanding of your company. If your firm is less well known, then that may be a signal that a vital aspect to your marketing communication should include educating the market.

Recommended Magic Numbers to Evaluate Market Awareness of Your Brand(s)

- **Brand Recall**

- **Brand Recognition**

Finally, a firm must review its current financial situation.

Recommended Magic Numbers to Review Financial Performance

- **Revenue**

- **Gross Profits**

- **Net Profits**

- **Profit Impact**

- **Earnings-Based Value**

- **Return on Sales**

- **Return on Assets**

- **Return on Equity**

- **Segment Profitability**

Strategy and Objectives

This section answers the question: where do we want to go? It includes the primary marketing, sales and financial *goals* (as opposed to the financial *review* conducted in the Situation Analysis). Strategy describes the primary directional elements of the marketing plan and most often includes target segments, customers, product lines and product positioning.

For a strategy to be realized, it has to be promoted, discussed and eventually accepted inside the rest of the company. Will everyone agree? No, nor should that be a criterion for confirming a strategy. But neither can it be conceived by one person and foisted upon others with the assumption that people will jump in line to support it. That may have worked during the dark ages of business when companies were run by dictatorial Neanderthals, but the rapid globalization of the past decade has increased options and job opportunities for business people. Now, if talented employees feel strangled by outdated "do it my way" thinking, they can easily change companies. But employee turnover is expensive and it is therefore incumbent on marketers to cooperate and network with other departments, managers and executives regularly to ensure that the marketing issues are understood and do not come as a surprise. Creating a plan and then handing it off to another department saying "Just do it" is not going to win you any favors, much less any support.

Recommended Magic Numbers for Assessing Market Potential

- **Market Coverage**

- **Market-Share Potential**

- **Market-Share Development Performance**

- **Market Demand**

- **Future Demand**

Recommended Magic Numbers to Forecast Financial Potential

- **Revenue**

- **Gross Profits**

- **Net Profits**

- **Profit Impact**

- **Earnings-Based Value**

- **Return on Sales**

- **Return on Assets**

- **Return on Equity**

- **Segment Profitability**

Action Plans and Marketing Programs

This section answers the question: how do we get there? Turning strategies into actions is central to success. This section outlines the programs marketing will implement, including promotions, advertising, cross-media schedules and pricing. Equally important, it describes who is responsible for the programs, what the deliverables are expected to be, how they will be delivered and key milestone dates.

In proposing their programs, marketers may decide to undertake more research before determining and implementing a course of action. Developing a market-research budget is helpful here.

Recommended Magic Number for Marketing Research

- **Market-Research Budget**

Evaluating marketing programs can be extensive and intensive, particularly for larger companies with complex strategies and tactics. You should first consider which programs are likely to be most effective in reaching your target audience. Therefore, while there are many Magic Numbers listed below, most marketing plans would not use *all* of these. Your specific Magic Number selections will depend on the nature of the marketing programs you select.

Recommended Magic Numbers for Evaluating Marketing Programs

- **Segment Profitability**

- **New-Product Purchase Rate**

- **Share of Customer**

- **Customer-Acquisition Cost**

- **Customer Break-Even Analysis**

- **Customer Lifetime-Value Analysis**
- **Loyalty**

Pricing

- **Price**
- **Premiums**
- **Marketing ROI (floor price)**
- **Mark-Up Price**
- **Target-Return Price**
- **Pricing Frameworks**

Advertising Measures

- **Share of Voice**
- **Advertising-to-Sales Ratio**
- **Reach**
- **Frequency**
- **Gross Rating Points**
- **Cost Per Gross Rating Point**
- **Click-Through Rates**
- **Profit Per Campaign**

Retail Measures

- **Turnover**
- **Gross Margin Return on Inventory Investment**
- **Sales Per Square Foot**
- **Sales/Profit Per Employee**
- **Average Transaction Size**

- **Average Items Per Transaction**
- **Retailer's Margin Percentage**

Direct Marketing Measures

- **Response Rate**
- **Conversion Rate**
- **Direct-Mail Revenue Goals**
- **Direct-Mail Profit Goals**
- **Direct-Mail Gross Profit**
- **Direct-Mail Net Profit**
- **Direct-Mail ROI**

Performance Monitoring

This section answers the question: how do we measure and, if necessary, change our performance? It is important to outline how the marketing plan, strategies and programs are to be measured. This may include assessment at predetermined dates following key program-launch and market-feedback cycles. Marketers will use these measures to periodically assess the health of their plan and determine where corrections are needed.

Recommended Magic Numbers for Monitoring Performance

Essentially, any of the Magic Numbers in the preceding section on Marketing Programs could also be used to monitor progress. For that matter, overall revenues, product sales targets, profitability measures, market share progress and more, can be used. The final choice is yours and depends on the strategic objectives of the company and the programs implemented.

Finding the Information

There are numerous online resources that marketers and those interested in learning more about marketing can use to add to their knowledge of marketing measures.

- **Marketing Science Institute (MSI)** www.msi.org

MSI was founded to bridge the gap between academia and industry. Through conferences, research and publishing, MSI regularly contributes a wide range of first-rate marketing research. Some of its materials are available as PDF downloads. Otherwise, you can order research papers by paying a fee per item. MSI also has membership opportunities, but you have to join and become a member company, or be an academic.

- **American Marketing Association (AMA)**
  www.marketingpower.com

This is a comprehensive site offering articles, business services and education programs. In it you will find the answers to most general marketing questions. To gain access to premium content, though, you must become a paying member.

- **MarketingProfs** www.marketingprofs.com

Its name is short for "Marketing Professors/Professionals", that is, people who make their career from marketing activities. Similar to the AMA in that it offers research and articles about marketing, as well as seminars and events. It tends to cater more toward the post-MBA audience, whereas the AMA appeals to a broader marketing audience. You must become a member to gain access to premium content, although a fair amount of research is available to non-members.

- **Brand Channel** www.brandchannel.com

Brandchannel.com is produced by Interbrand, a global brand consultancy. It offers articles, research papers, books and well-organized surveys, all with respect to learning about and disseminating information on global brands.

- *AdWeek Magazine* www.adweek.com

AdWeek is a publication, online and offline, of VNU, a publishing company that also produces *BrandWeek* (www.brandweek.com) and *MediaWeek* (www.mediaweek.com), all three of which offer the latest news in their respective industry segments.

- *AdAge Magazine* www.adage.com

Similar to *AdWeek*, this is an industry publication with articles and information on the latest activities in the world of advertising.

- *McKinsey Quarterly* www.mckinseyquarterly.com

McKinsey is a well-known global strategy consultancy. You can subscribe to its quarterly publication, which offers a wide range of content, including marketing and branding topics.

- *Harvard Business Review* www.hbsp.com

One of several publications from Harvard Business School Publishing, this offers articles on a wide range of business topics, including marketing.

- **Direct Marketing Association** www.the-dma.org

Similar to the AMA, this site offers publications, education programs and an active members network.

Other Publications

The following publications often have useful articles about marketing and branding:

- *Fast Company* www.fastcompany.com

- *Business 2.0* www.business2.com

- *BusinessWeek* www.businessweek.com

- *Fortune* www.fortune.com

- *Sales and Marketing Management* www.salesandmarketing.com

- *Sloan Management Review* www.sloanreview.mit.edu/edu/smr

- *California Management Review* www.haas.berkeley.edu/News/cmr

- *Journal of Marketing* www.marketingjournals.com

Each of the following periodicals may be found at the American Marketing Association website, www.marketingpower.com, under the link "AMA Publications".

- *Journal of Marketing Research* www.marketingpower.com (same as American Marketing Association)

- *Journal of International Marketing* www.marketingpower.com

- *Marketing Management* www.marketingpower.com

- *Marketing News* www.marketingpower.com

Other Global Marketing Organizations

Australian Marketing Institute www.ami.org.au

Chartered Institue of Marketing www.cim.co.uk/cim

Japan Marketing Association www.jma-jp.org/

Marketing Institute of Singapore www.mis.org.sg/

Index

Other Titles in the MAG1C NUM8ERS Series...

An excellent reference guide to the key quantitative assessment tools for HR practitioners. This book simply outlines a range of the key measures that any HR, financial or business manager can use to address this situation in a more business-like manner.

0-470-82161-2
October 2005

This book looks at key ratios that all investors can use easily to look at the financial health and growth prospects of a company before they buy shares in it. The ratios are described in details, with simple formulas, and help on where to find the data needed to calculate them.

0-470-82124-8
September 2003

Magic Numbers is the essential guide to making objective judgements about companies and their shares. If you don't want to see your money cut in half or vanish altogether, we strongly recommend you read this book.

0-471-47924-1
August 2001

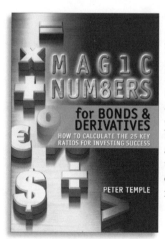

With investment choices becoming broader, savvy investors need to know not just about stocks, but also about bonds and derivatives. This book is the first real attempt to explain the inner workings of these alternative investment choices.

0-470-82139-6
November 2004